Celtic Patterns for Beginners

Abby O'Shea

Table of Contents

Introduction

Humans' love and admiration for aesthetics permeate back hundreds of thousands of years. Humans across the world have created objects to symbolize their cultures, beliefs, interests, and other life areas, just for pleasure. What they did then was just for fun. Little did they know that they were laying the foundation for the birth of art. During the Middle Ages, Celtic Art, often considered as the ancient inhabitants of Britain and Ireland, was born. It was believed that Celtic art was practiced as early as the 5th century. Celts' art, also known as Celtic art, focused mainly on ornamental artistry made up of patterns, knots, foliage, spirals, and animals. These ornamental designs were mainly symbols of natural elements such as water, air, fire, and other spiritual entities. Celts were busy migrating from one place to the other because of the ongoing wars of the Iron Age. So, they learned so many things about the cultures of the places they visited and incorporated those cultures in their art.

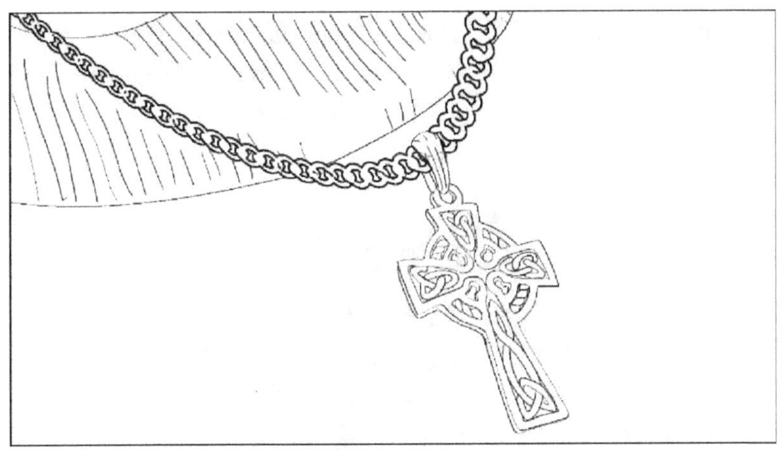

The constant wars of the period aided the spread of Celtic art across distant lands. Celts migrated and changed locations at the time, and other people had access to their rich cultural heritage. Celts' belief in superstition was second to none at the time. And, since it was a period people had so much respect and reverence for superstition and religion, everyone was eager to learn the Celts' way of life. So, just before anyone knew what was going on, Celtic art had won the people's hearts and minds. Of course, no one could turn down the beauty of Celtic designs, even if they wanted to. Humans continue to enjoy Celtic masterpiece designs from pendants to rings, necklaces, tattoos, and other ornamental designs. Civilization might have shaped the kinds of knots being produced, but the Celtic culture remains intact.

Anyone who's determined and committed to learning the processes of Celtic art can create impressive Celtic knots. What if I don't have previous knowledge of art? No worries. You can learn the techniques. Again, this book uses easy-to-understand words to describe the process of creating excellent knots. So, you can learn the process from scratch once you're determined and committed.

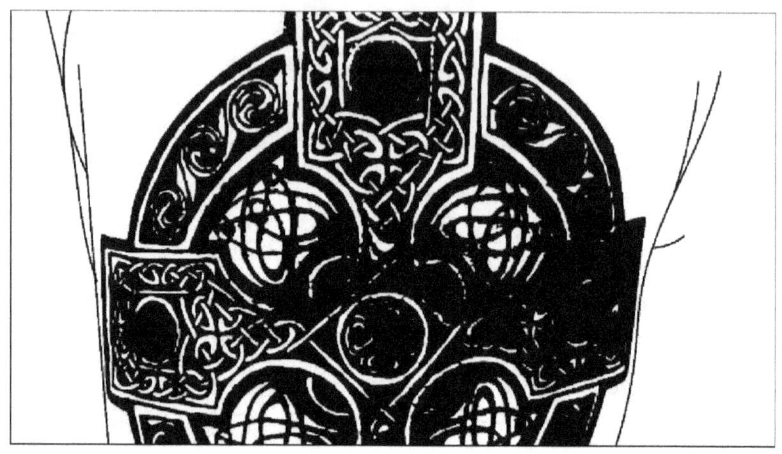

A career in Celtic art is full of positives. It is a platform to light up your creativity. Celtic art will open your eyes to innovative ways to light up your imagination. So, rather than idling your creativity, you can channel it into designing a fantastic Celtic pattern that will amaze many people. Also, it can show you a clearer picture of the world. A look at some Celtic designs and their supposed meanings will open your eyes to the realities of the world, and you'll learn so many things about other people's cultures and traditions through drawings. Still, Celtic art could be a path to fulfilling your passion. A career in Celtic art may not fetch you huge pay, but it could be an opportunity to follow your passion. Sure, it is something you'll love doing as soon as you get started.

What am I going to learn in this book?

So many amazing things to learn! Chapter one digs deep into the evolution of Celtic arts and the issues that aided the spread of the art during the Medieval period, while chapter two presents the gallery of beautiful Celtic ornaments and designs. Chapter three and four explains braids, twists, knotted lines, and Celtic patterns, with so many tips and tricks on how you can create your own designs at the comfort of your home.

Chapter five takes you through layout ideas and how to create one for your Celtic design. In chapter six, you will learn how to enhance your Celtic pattern with color, while chapter seven's focus is line enhancements. You may be dreaming of creating a unique and highly decorative Celtic design now. Great! Chapter eight offers the help you need to create a Celtic knot decorated, while chapter nine captures Celtic pattern knotted coasters.

Just name your questions. 'Celtic Patterns for Beginners' captures everything about Celtic art—yes, everything you need to be an established Celtic artist. Read, digest, and follow the techniques discussed in this book to create amazing Celtic patterns.

Chapter One: Introduction to Celtic Art

Celtic arts and crafts first hit Iron Age Europe around 1000 BCE, following a group of Celts migrating from Southern Russia. Early Celt migrants, who settled in the Upper Danube area, absorbed Ancient Danubian motifs and came with their cultural styles, including strings of knowledge from the Caucasian Bronze Age and the Mediterranean Etruscan styles. Still, they had vast experience in metalwork, jewelry art, and iron making. Their jewelry art, which was next to none at the time, could be from Russia's Caucasus' Bronze-making Maikop or as a result of Celts' early contact with the Levant. For example, the Gundestrup cauldron, Celts' masterpiece silver jewelry, was believed to hit the Black Sea region.

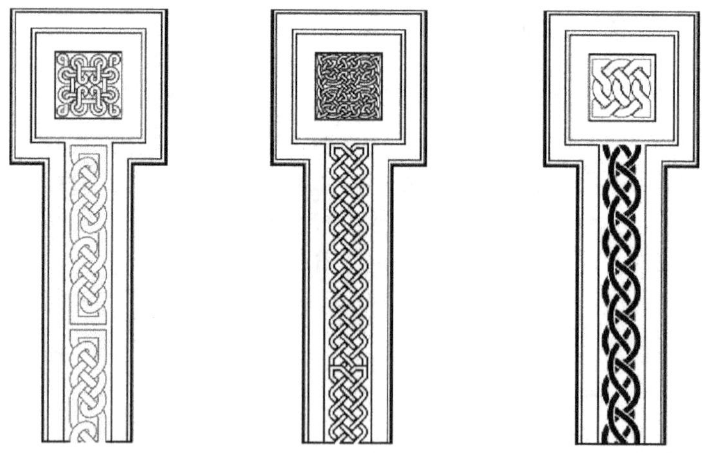

Celtic Art deals with lots of geometric shapes, and it covers several ornamental artistic designs such as patterns, spirals, and foliage. Following the revivalist movement to advance Celtic designs, the tentacles of Celtic Art were extended to cover other techniques and embellishments such as paintings, wall stenciling, stain glass, and different architectural designs. Ancient Celts were wealthy, intelligent, and complicated people. They were polytheists and very superstitious. Historically, most of them were farmers and warriors, and they lived on high mountains, where they could reverence natural elements such as the sun, the moon, the stars, and the Earth. Celts people believe that these natural elements could shape the course of their lives, either for good or bad. Apart from these natural elements, early Celtic Art designs also centered on another seven elements— plants, fish, reptiles, insects, birds, mammals, and humans.

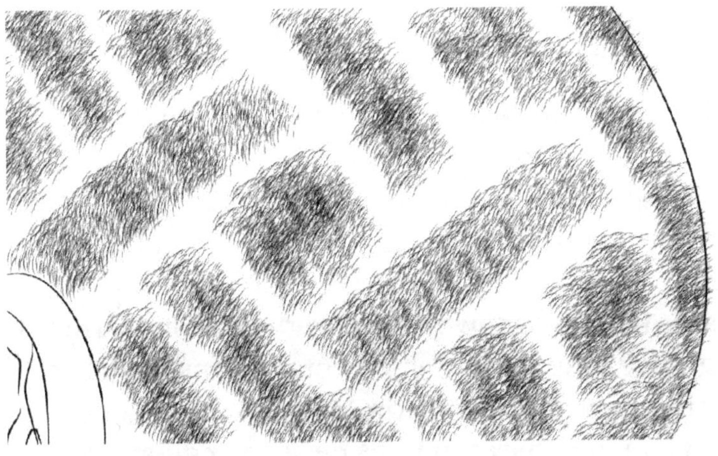

The Birth of Celtic Art

Historians contend that the Caucasians influenced early Celts during the Bronze Age. They believe that Celts' initial contact with the Caucasians helped them understand how to design iron and jewelry. Those things took center stage then. However, since the Celts traded with people close to the Mediterranean and the Black Sea, they might have been influenced by other art styles and cultures.

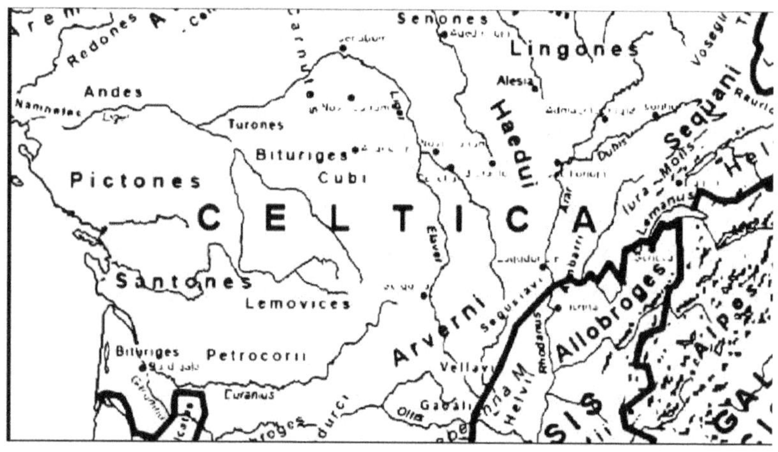

Still, the Celts learned a few things from the Danubian tradition. Artists soon learned to discard the classical tradition of Celtic Art by trading with people from other climes. Expectedly, the cultures and traditions of those people began to shape Celtic Arts. These influences snowballed into the various forms of designs we now see in Celtic knot patterns, scrollwork, letterings, and spirals. Celtic Art might have gone through many phases, but it's designs and patterns have always retained its intricate sense of balance.

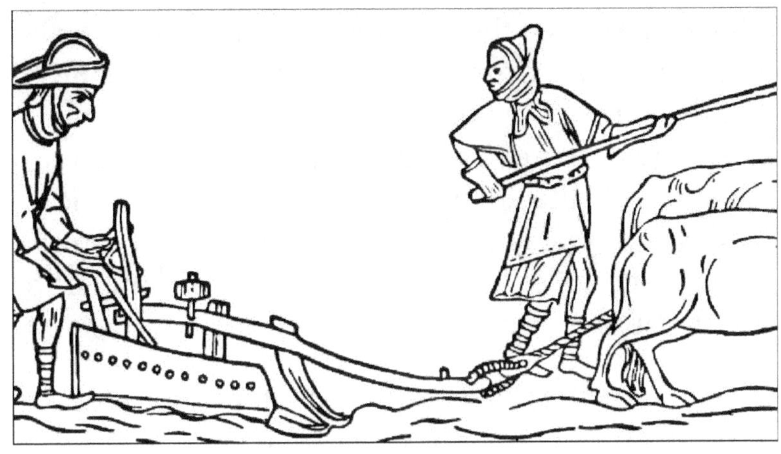

Celtic artists know how to balance positive and negative spaces to harmonize the message they intend to drive home. They try to elaborate their lines and curves to curb surface, vessel, and material irregularities, especially when they try to carve or draw Celtic patterns.

Early Celtic Art and La Tene

Nothing stood out in the early phase of Celtic Art more than its geometrical designs, lovely spirals, and charming active circles. Yet, those patterns and designs were previously unknown to Celtic Art. They were mostly wood carvings and metal sculptures from La Tene, a defunct region in present-day Switzerland. La Tene was the center of Iron Age culture in old Europe. Swirling curvilinear patterns and ornamental motifs were the standout designs of the Iron Age, and Artists in La Tene actively designed so many jewelry accessories with gold, bronze, iron, and other precious metals.

They also used these patterns to embellish their weapons, bowls, trumpets, cauldrons, and drinking vessels. Remember I told you that early Celts were mostly fighters and farmers. What we know as Celtic Art today is quite different from what was available hundreds of years before. Celtic Twilight, also known as the modern Celtic Art revival, has refined the Art to suit the present age.

The revival birthed a renewed interest in Celtic Art in the middle of the 19th century and paved the way for brooches and other unique Celtic designs. Also, Celtic motifs became dominant in architectural designs at this period. Still, knots, interlaced birds, whorls, and geometric designs, like other amazing Celtic art designs, flourished during this period.

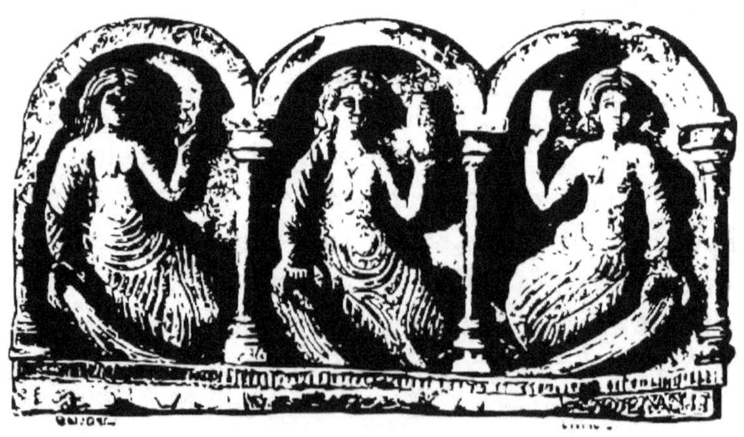

Celtic Knot Patterns

Celts were very religious and superstitious. They attached spiritual and superstitious meanings to most

of their designs if not all. For example, Celtic
mythology held that knots symbolized sacred
geometry that connected life to the universe. Celtic
knot patterns may vary, but they all represent one
spiritual or superstitious thing or the other.
Historians believe that Celtic knot patterns dated back
to 450 A.D. when Christianity began to influence
Celtic civilization. Some of these knot patterns, which
symbolized love, friendship, faith, and loyalty, were
used to design early Christian artworks and
manuscripts.

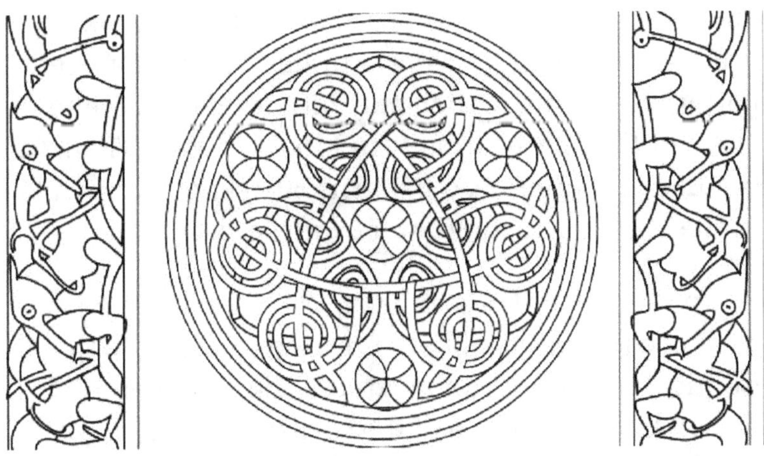

Still, intricate patterns were used, and still being
used, to decorate items such as cutlery, clothing,
plates, jewelry, and mugs. Some of these items are
used daily, but many people still don't understand the
symbolism and spirituality attached to these Celtic
knot patterns. Regular Celtic knot patterns include the
cross, trinity, tree of life, shield, heart, and spiral
knots. Others are knotwork interlace, step patterns,

and dara knots. Chapter Two captures all these knots, their meanings, and how you can create them.

Historical Overview of Interlocking and Interlacing Line Designs and Patterns

Interlace, a decorative art form in medieval Art, was a common visual art in the Iron Age. Artists looped and knotted bands and motifs to create complex geometric patterns. Those patterns were used to fill empty spaces in created designs. Norse Art of the Iron Age, Islamic Art, Insular Art of Ireland, and the Migration Art of Northern Europe extensively utilized interlacing. Intricate braided and interlaced patterns later made their way into Roman Art in many areas in Europe, especially in Mosaic floors. Then, the braided and interlaced patterns, also known as plaits in the United Kingdom, were widespread.

In the 5th and 6th century, Christians in Egypt used broad-strand ribbon interlace to decorate their Coptic manuscripts and textiles. The ornamental design looked like one of the earliest knotworks of insular Art. Yes, the insular Art of Ireland, as well as that of the British Isles.

Northern Europe was not left out. The Migration Period saw the birth of Style II, the animal style decoration. Interlace was at the center of this decoration, and it hit most parts of Northern Europe. Lombards eventually took the design to Northern Italy. The long ribbons of Style II terminated on the head of an animal. By 700 CE, the animal style decoration had begun to fade out in several areas in Europe, unlike Scandinavia and the British Isles.

In those areas, interlace was extensively used in woodcarving, metalwork, high crosses, runestones, and illuminated manuscripts. This development continued for five centuries—the 7th to 12th centuries. George Bain is an artist. He went through the Durham Cathedral Gospel Book and the Book of Durrow, books written in the 7th century. Having characterized the insular knotwork in the two books, George Bain found that broken and rejoined braids were extensively used. Still, no one knows how Coptic braid patterns got to the Hiberno-Scottish monasteries. But people tend to believe that the practices might have migrated from Lombardic Art in Italy or that of the Eastern Mediterranean.

James Johnson, an art historian, looked at it from another angle. He argued that the Coptic monasteries of Egypt and the Scriptoria of Early Christian in Ireland, being decorative interlace arts, deserved attention. Highlights of these two designs were their symmetrically-shaped and intertwined elongated beasts. Again, this design style dated back to the 7th century, and it is similar to the Hop and Sutton treasure. The Viking Age art, centered on the Urnes style, had the largest interlaced zoomorphic, and it dated as far back as 1050. The striking point of the Viking Age art was its stylized animals and intertwined tendrils of foliate designs.

The British Isles' insular Art activated the full flowering of interlace in Northern Europe. Style II, Northern Europe's animal style ornament, was blended with ribbon knotwork designs found in the Cross of Cong and the Book of Kells, two great books of the time. Christian activities strongly influenced those books. Interlace was used to illuminate carpet pages and other notable designs of the time. Soon, insular interlace found its way into continental Europe and was extensively used between the 8th and 11th centuries. Franco-Saxon school and Carolingian schools of illumination, like other notable schools of the time, utilized interlace in their foliate decorative designs. Also, Romanesque Art was no different. Less complex interlace patterns and animal designs were found.

Interlace patterns formed the highlight of Islamic Art. Islamic ornament had lots of geometric interlacing patterns. Most of these patterns fell under arabesque designs and were evident in Umayyad architecture designs such as cravings and wall paintings, mosaics, decorative metalwork, and window grilles. Such techniques took center stage in Islamic Art between the 8th and 10th centuries but later paved the way for the intricate interlacing patterns of medieval Islamic Art. Kufic calligraphy also had some interlaced elaborations.

Southern Europe, just like the Northern part, had its fair share in the historical evolution of interlacing. Byzantine Art, the region's known design, was impacted by interlace and knotwork, although with little or no prominence. Three-ribbon, the only notable example of interlace in the area, was found in Croatia in the early medieval period. The interlace was carved on stone between the 9th and 11 centuries.

Chapter Summary

- Celtic art hit Iron Age Europe in 1000 BCE.

- It covers ornamental artistic designs as spirals and foliage and can be used for geometric shapes.

- The tentacles of Celtic art can be extended to other forms of designs and embellishments.

In the next chapter, you will learn a few things about Celtic art Gallery.

Chapter Two:
Gallery

We already considered the meaning and history of Celtic arts and patterns in the last chapter. Let's take a step further to see a few examples of Celtic designs and create some projects. So, one after the other, let us run through these Celtic patterns. Celtic knots are usually bold, adorable, and appealing, but they all have unique meanings, all parts of the Celtic heritage. Each Celtic symbol has a particular purpose or message, although this meaning may vary across cultures.

Today, we will go back to history to study these Celtic symbols and their meanings carefully. So, sit comfortably, relax while I take you around the world of Celtic symbols.

Trinity Knot

The Trinity knot is also known as Triquetra. It was the symbol of the Mother, Maiden, and Crone, a famous Celts' goddess. It is one of the most popular Celtic characters.

The Trinity knot is highly symbolic and has a deep spiritual meaning, especially among the Irish. For some, it is believed to be a symbol of the 'Holy Trinity' representing God – The Father, The Son, and The Holy Spirit.

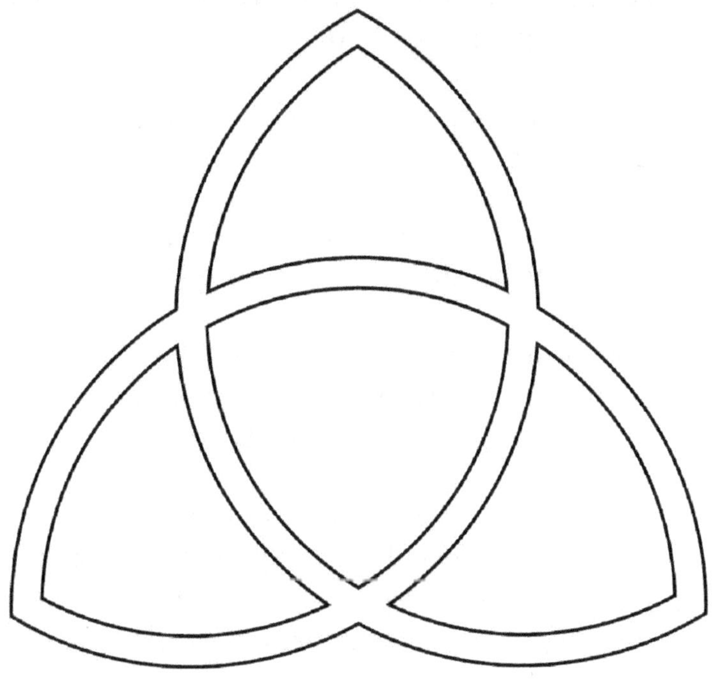

In Christendom, especially among Catholics, representations of the Trinity knot are found on paintings and artworks on the church walls. Among neo-pagan worshippers, the Trinity knot also holds significance. It signifies the three-life cycles of womanhood in relation (Youth, Motherhood, and Old Age) to the moon's phases – past, present, and future.

The Trinity Knot is a typical Celtic design replicated on jewelry, artwork, and other medieval art forms. The Celtic Trinity Knot is worn by many Irish as a symbol of never-ending love or ancestry.

You should also know that the Trinity Knot holds several meanings, and some of these include:

- The Trinity knot is also referred to as the Irish Love Knot.

- As a gift, it connotes a wish of the longevity of life to the receiver.

- According to ancient beliefs, Trinity Knot also symbolizes the three phases of a woman: Youth, Motherhood, and Old age.

- The endless intertwining curves found in most Trinity knots usually symbolizes everlasting love and is an excellent gift for engagements, weddings, and marriage anniversaries.

- The Trinity knot also symbolizes the three circles of life: life, death, and rebirth.

- It also represents the husband's marital vows to his wife: love, honor, and protection.

- It also symbolizes the moon phases, which has to do with time - past, present, and future; or the family structure representing the father, mother, and children.

- It is a representation of ancient Irish culture.

Celtic Self-Contained Patterns

These are twists, braids, and knot patterns created using one continuous line to create an aesthetic Celtic design. Celtic self-contained patterns are usually without a beginning or end, i.e., there is no starting or finishing point on a Celtic knot. These are mainly used for decorations.

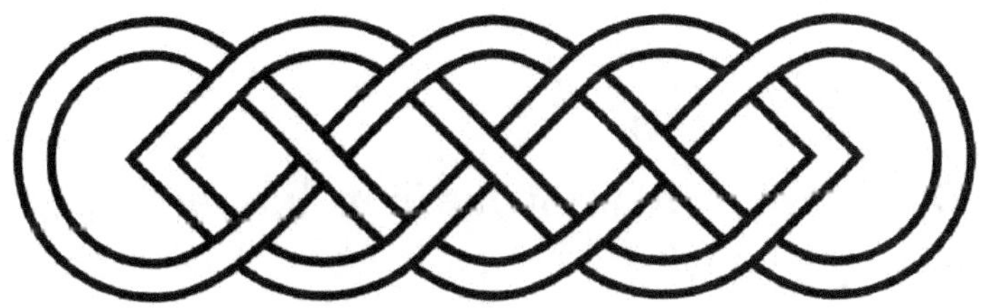

Celtic step patterns and critical patterns are prevalent motifs found in ancient Celtic arts right before the Christian influence on the Celts. However, these Celtic designs found their way into early Christian manuscripts and artwork.

Step patterns are also known as maze patterns and were found in ancient Egypt, Aztec, and Mayan art. It can symbolize progression and motion. It could also connote the spiritual relationship between heaven and earth.

Some of these artworks, in addition to depictions from life, such as animals, plants, and even humans, have been replicated over time by famous artists and painters.

Cutting Instructions (cut in the order listed)

- White/green print (background

- 4 rectangles 3½" x 6½"

- 1 square 3½" x 3½"

- 4 squares 2" x 2"

Dark green swirl print, medium lime mottle, light green floral, and dark green texture (links)—cut from each:

- 1 strip 2" x 5"

- 1 rectangle 2" x 3½"

- 3 squares 2" x 2"

Piecing the Block.

1. Sew together 1 white/green print 2" square, 1 dark green swirl print 2" square, and 1 medium lime mottle 2" x 3½" rectangle to make pieced square.

2. Make 4 total in fabric arrangements shown.

3. Draw a diagonal line on the wrong side of lime 2" square. Place marked square on white/green 3½" x 6½" rectangle, right sides together, aligning raw edges.

4. Stitch on the drawn line and trim away.

Celtic Spiral Knot

The Celtic Spiral Knot is a representation of infinity, and it symbolizes unity and union of spirit. It represents the human journey from the physical to spiritual life/phase.

The Spiral Knot was mostly found at graveyards, often engraved on tombs. Thus, it is thought to be a symbol of the human transition from life to death.

The most common type of Spiral Knot that you'd find is the Triple Spiral Knot, which is also a trinity design, and three connecting spirals often represent it. They represent the water, fire, and earth, which are the driving force of nature.

Types of Celtic Spirals

Single Spiral

You may not know, but the single spiral is one of the most common Celtic symbols found on monuments and other artifacts. It holds different meanings, and for some people, it could stand for growth, equity, affinity, order, and development.

For others, it could represent the mind's journey from a materialistic world to an astronomical/cosmic world. It is also a competent representation of knowledge, experiences, and mindfulness.

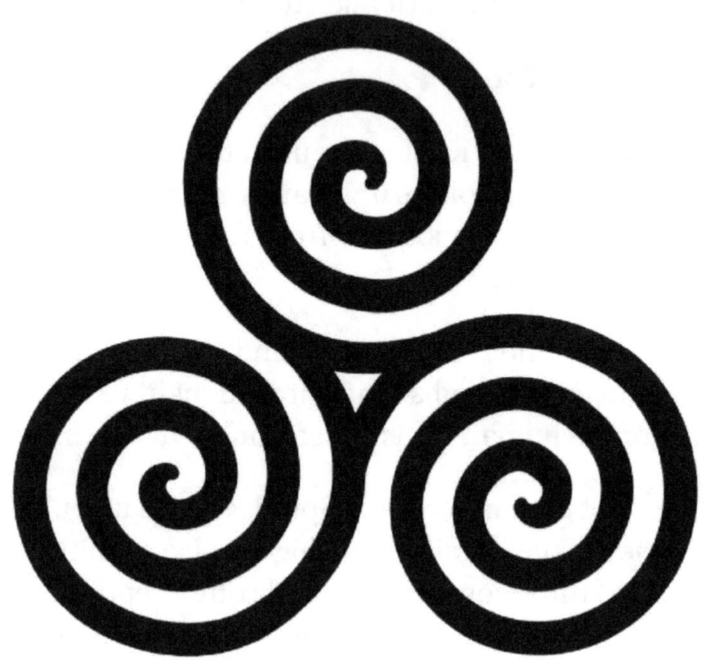

Double Spiral

The Double Spiral is a clockwise movement of two points on a line that forms the double spiral. Just like the single spiral, it also has various meanings for different people. According to ancient beliefs, the double spiral symbolizes the sun and its double spiral movement, which happens over a year.

It could also represent balance and is also a symbol that represents man's creation and destruction, human birth, death, and a profound spiritual awakening.

Triple Spiral

Also referred to as the Triple Spiralis, the Triple Spiral is an ancient Celtic symbol that became very popular in 500BC. The versatility of the triple spiral meanings cannot be overemphasized; although it depends on the context and culture, it is used.

It could represent progress, revolution, movement, cycle, etc. It could also stand for the soul, body, and mind. Also, it symbolizes intellect, love, and power. It also represents the physical, spiritual, and cosmic world.

Celtic Love Knot

This type of Celtic knot, also called the Trikeles, represents undying and everlasting love between two people. The Celtic Love knot is also referred to as the Anam Cara Knot. From the Irish words meaning soul friend, it was recently added to the list of Celtic Knots.

Here, two Celtic knot hearts are intertwined to form one infinite loop, and it is a modern acclimation of the classic Celtic knot. One thing you should know is that the pattern found on the Celtic Love Knot is infinite.

It is common among lovers and is used to represent a relationship of everlasting love. You can find most lovers wearing rings with the Love knot pattern, and in ancient marriage rites, lovers exchanged this knot instead of rings.

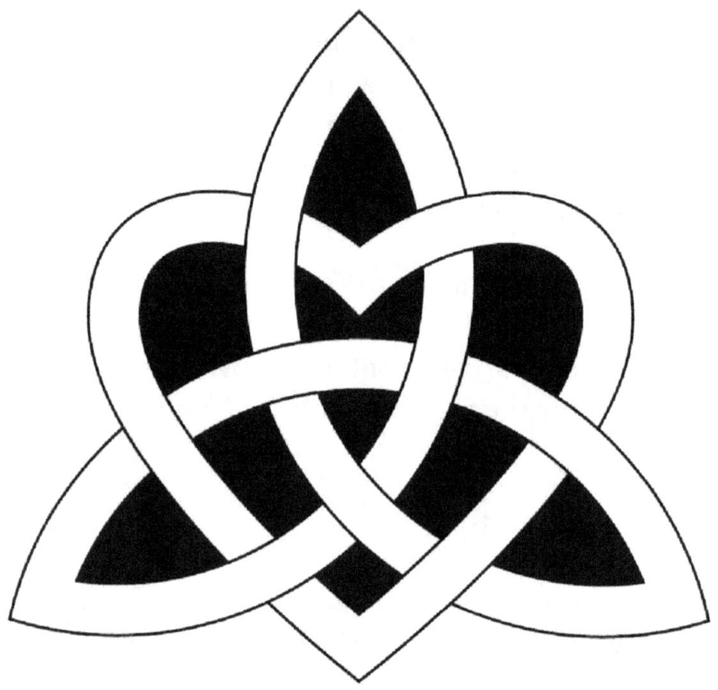

Celtic Cross

The Celtic Cross stands for the four elements and directions according to ancient legends. The Celtic Cross was and is still highly a religious and spiritual symbol. The Celtic ornate cross holds a lot of meaning for both pagans and Christians.

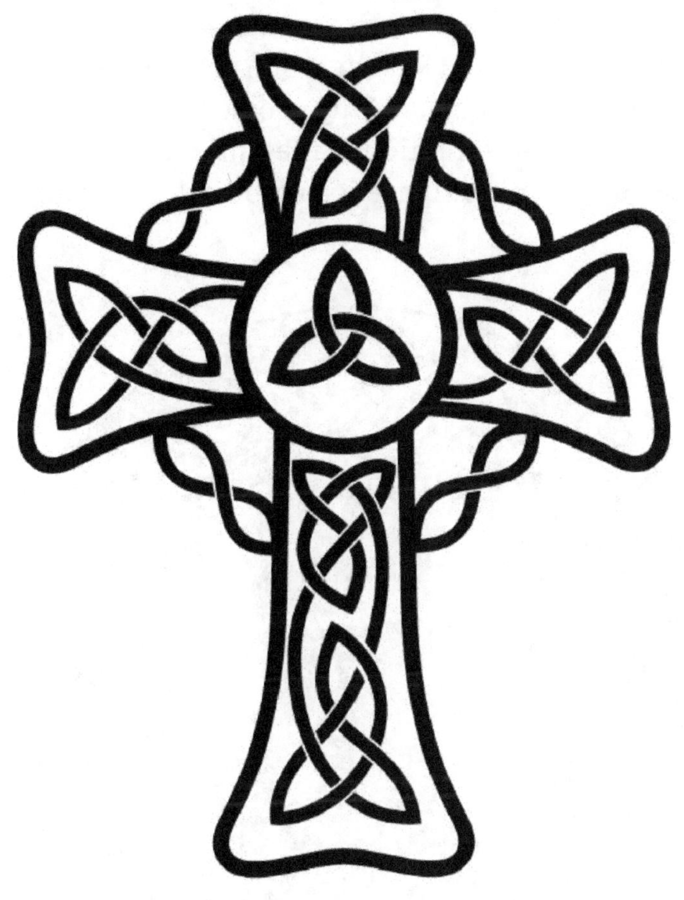

For pagans, the circle found at the center of the cross references the Sun God in ancient times. On the other hand, Christians believe that the cross was where Jesus Christ, the son of God, died for our sins; hence, it symbolizes God's love, which is eternal.

Round Celtic Design

The Round Celtic Design is one of the most popular Celtic symbols. Many people believe that the symbol is a representation of the Christian teachings of the Holy Trinity. Hence it connotes the unity of spirit.

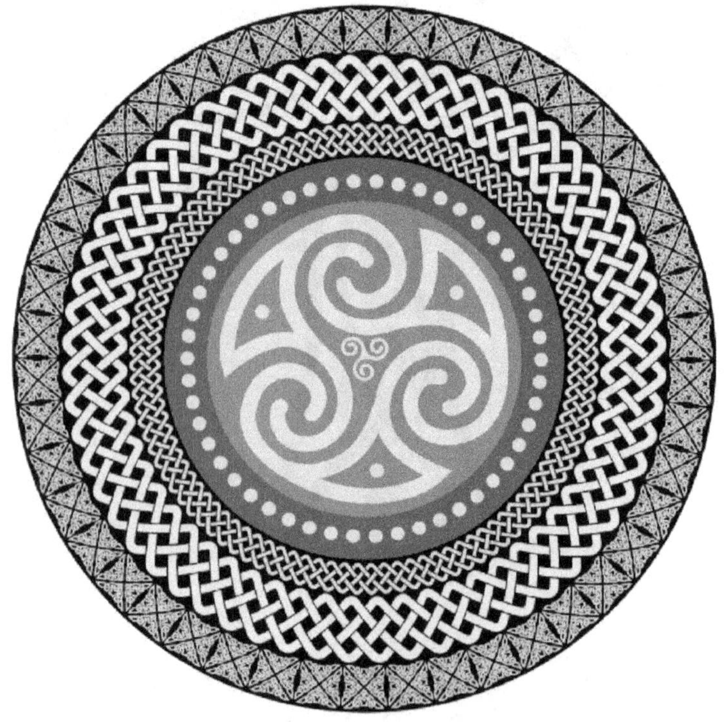

Among Christians, there is the belief that the circle symbolizes God's never-ending love and a representation of the cycle of life, which is birth, death, and rebirth. It also stands for loyalty, friendship, and love, although these meanings may vary among different cultures.

Frame Corner

The Frame corner is also a well-known Celtic design that is very aesthetic. It is an ancient Celtic design made on frames for embellishments. A frame corner doesn't have any known meaning or symbolism; however, it is a modern addition to the collection of classic Celtic designs and patterns.

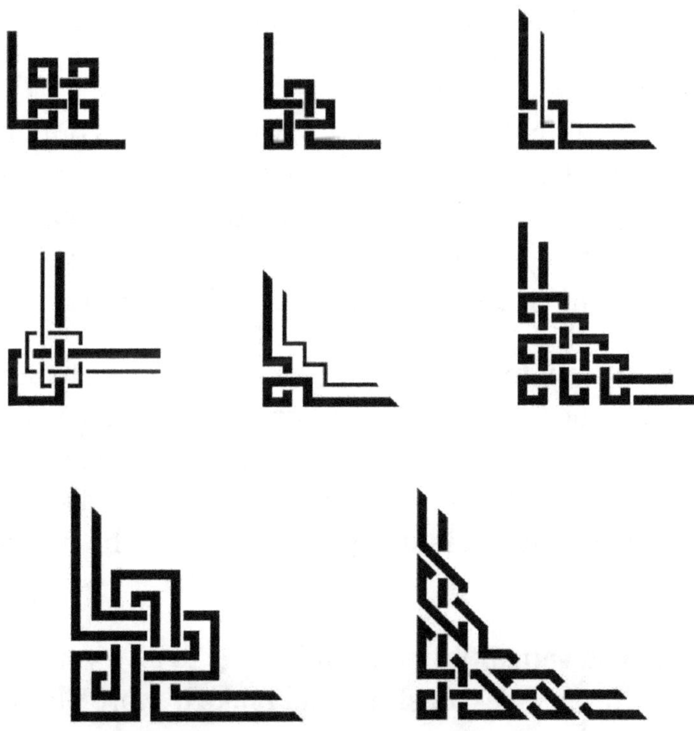

To create a Celtic frame corner is relatively easy once you follow guidelines thoroughly. You need to get your glue, quick clamps, a poplar board, glazier points, wood stain, straight router and round bit, miter saw, and a flush-trim saw.

Here are the guidelines on how to create your frame corner:

1. Using a 1x4 poplar board, cut out 4 boards and rip them down to 3 inches each.

2. Make accurate cuts on your boards by using your miter saw set to 45 degrees.

3. After making your cut, lay your boards out and check for errors. Once that is done, apply your glue to each board and join them together, making sure they're all square and clamped tightly together using your quick clamps.

4. After applying the glue, you can choose to add corner splines to your board. To do this, you make use of a DIY spline jig and a contrasting wood. Cut out another set of poplar boards, add glue, and push your spline into the boards' joints.

5. You can apply wood finishings to give your frame an extra shine and make it more pleasing to the eyes.

6. Trim off rough edges and extra wood using your flush trim saw.

7. Assemble your frame by using glazier points to hold everything in place, especially when screwing your corner splines. You should screw every 6 inches (a bit more or less) using a Flathead screwdriver.

Just like that, you have completed the Celtic frame corner.

Square Knot

The square knot is also known as the shield knot. It was an ancient Celtic Knot that was worn by warriors for protection in times of war. Ill people also used it to ward off illness and evil spirits, and danger.

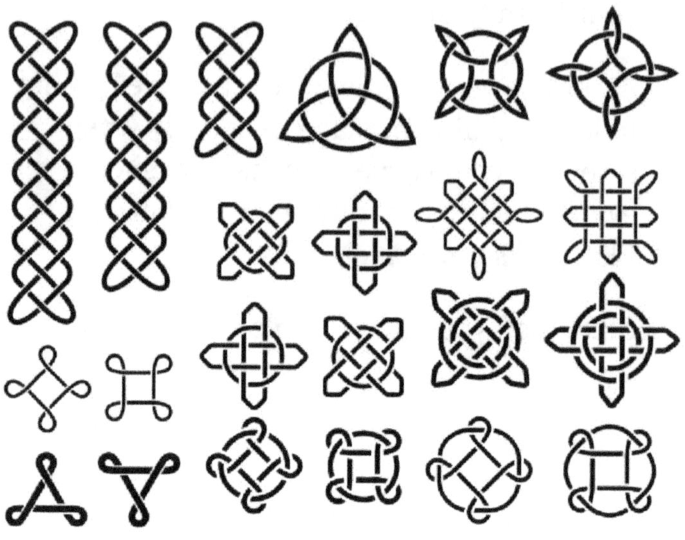

You can recreate the Square or shield knot in various designs. However, you must include its four corners to make it a square knot. The square knot comprises heavily-made patterns that are tight to depict an unbreakable barrier.

The shield knot has a lot of complex meanings. It can symbolize the elements of nature, which are earth, wind, fire, and water. Also, it represents St. Brigid's four tiers of wisdom, i.e., heart, head, hearth, and hand.

The square knot represents good fortune and prosperity and the four unique Celtic festivals - Imbolic, Samhain, Lughnasadh, and Bealtaine.

Circular Knot

Circular knots usually come in different designs, although one thing they share in common is that they are all circular. Circular knots often symbolizes the continuity of human life and also purity and wholeness.

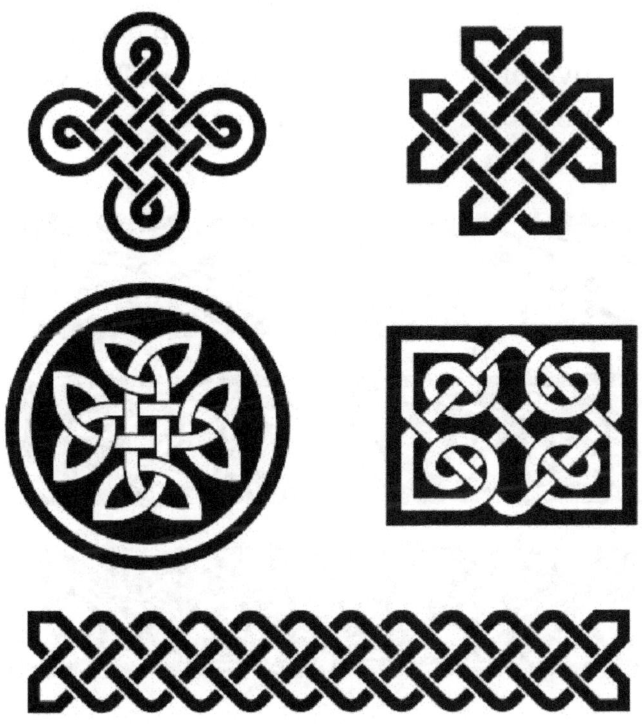

There is no beginning or end in circular knots, which is common among almost all Celtic knots. The Dara knot, which is almost like a maze, is an example of a Celtic circular knot, and they symbolize leadership, power, wisdom, and strength. Dara's name comes from the Irish word 'Doire,' meaning oak tree, which represents strength.

Knot Birds Designs

Animals were an essential part of Celtic folklore and mythology. Ancient Celtic legends often associated animals with motion, fertility, and vitality. Out of all the animals, the most common one depicted in Celtic mythology and arts was the Bird. The Celts had a peculiar connection with birds.

When you come across most images of ancient Celtic and Druid gods, you see that the artist depicted these gods holding birds in their hands who acted as divine servants.

In ancient Celtic arts and beliefs, birds symbolized skill, knowledge, and, weirdly, bloodshed. Hence, old Celtic artists drew on the shields of most Celtic warriors and other emblems. The most commonly depicted birds are the swan, crow, and raven, although other animals were not left out. Old Celtic chiefs believed these birds were divine messengers of the gods, and because of this, they were revered.

The crow and raven usually represented bloodshed and battle, as well as connoting prophecy too. The Celtic 'triple' goddess, Morrigan, who controlled fertility, birth, and even death, is associated with the raven. The Celts used the raven to symbolize the death of slain warriors and also depict darkness. Even in modern movies and art, the raven still has a dark undertone and meaning to it, as you must have noticed.

The knot bird design holds different meanings. In ancient times, the Celts used birds to describe a warrior's fighting skills and prowess. It is also used to depict strength and was popular in ancient times.

Solomon's Knot

It is a Celtic symbol that represents man's connection to the divine. It is associated with King Solomon and reminiscent of many ancient civilizations apart from the Celts.

Awen Knot

It symbolizes creative inspiration and is associated with the poet, Bards.

Brigid's Cross

Early Christians named Brigid's cross after St. Brigid. People used Brigid's cross as a form of protection from evil spirits and danger. In Ireland, the Brigid cross also symbolizes the beginning of spring.

The Sailor's Knot

Ancient Celtic sailors weaved this to remember the loved ones they had left at home. It also represents everlasting love.

Celtic Tree of Life

The Celtic Tree of Life is a symbol of strength, balance, and harmony. The Celts believed that the dead lived in trees when they died, so they revered trees because it was a link between the living and the dead.

Chapter Summary

- Trinity knot is the symbol of The Mother, Maiden, and Crone.

- It symbolizes everlasting love and can be given to someone who's special to you.

The next chapter captures braids, twists, and knotted lines. Hope to see you there soon!

Chapter Three:
Introduction to Braids, Twists, and Knotted Lines

Braids, twists and knotted lines add beauty to quilts. They make our designs attractive and adorable. In this chapter, we will look at some of them and try to create some.

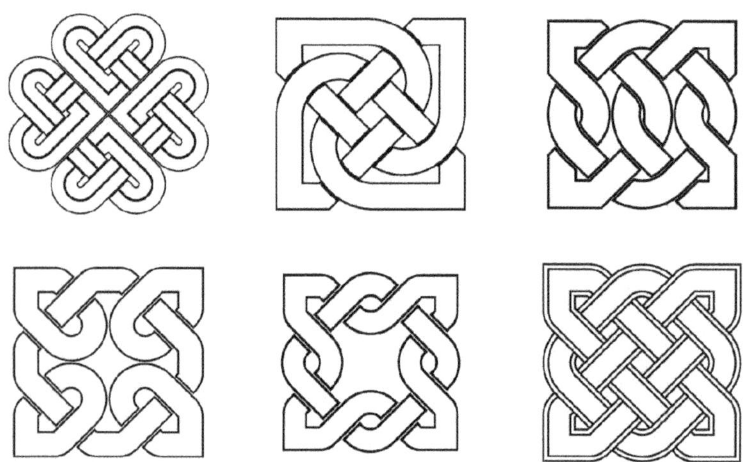

How to Draw a Celtic Cross

The Celtic Cross can be used to design beautiful pendants, jewelry, and rings, apart from other notable projects. Most often, and because of its spiritual undertone, Christians tend to use items decorated with this Cross more than other religious adherents. Why? The Celtic cross symbolizes the Cross on which

Jesus Christ was crucified. Here, I will teach you how to draw the Cross at the comfort of your home.

Required Materials

- Graph or grainy paper

- Pencil and eraser

- Pen or marker

- Ruler

Instructions

Follow these simple steps to draw your own Celtic Cross.

Step 1: Start by sketching the circle that will frame the center of the knot.

Step 2: Sketch a small circle that corresponds with the initial sketch.

Step 4: Sketch another smaller circle in the center of the already drawn circles

Step 5: Sketch the limbs of the Celtic knot. Sketch a set of parallel bent lines that deviate from one another on the side of the smallest center circle.

Join these lines on each end to make a scalloped style by linking numerous slight bent lines. Sketch a little L-shaped line above the center of each limb.

Step 6: Then, sketch two lines up and down. Again, make sure the line is curved and deviates from one another. Join the line at the base with a scalloped line.

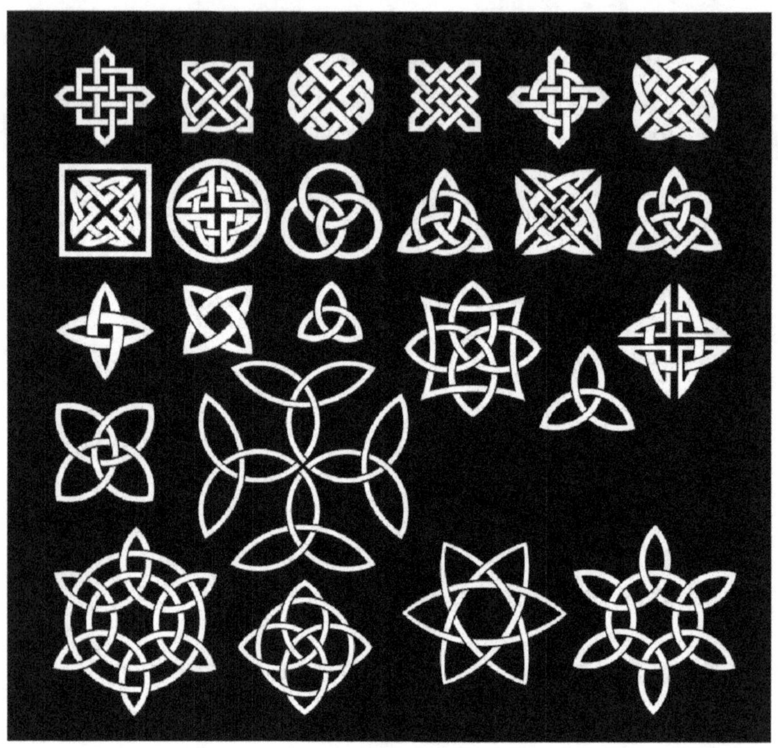

How to Draw a Trinity Knot

Trinity knot looks beautiful and charming. It is the perfect knot for Christians since it symbolizes 'The Father, The Son, and The Holy Spirit.' The knot has been extensively used to create lots of beautiful projects like rings, pendants, and necklaces. Also, these projects are what you can design in the comfort of your home once you know how to draw the trinity knot. No worries. Here, I will guide you on how you can draw your own trinity knot.

Required Materials

- Graph paper

- Pencil

- An eraser

- Pen or marker

- Ruler

Instructions

Follow these simple steps to draw your own trinity knot.

Step 1: Draw a separating line, and place a dot at the lower part of left and right. Place another dot at the upper part of the left and right.

Step 2: Sketch a big curve beginning from the top dot, curving to the right of the separator, then move over to the left-hand dot.

Step 3: Sketch another curve from the top dot, downward to the left of the separator, and then over to the right-hand dot.

Step 4: Connect the left and right dots with a curve bent to the top in the center. Thus, the outside shape of the trinity knot is complete.

Step 5: Now sketch another trinity knot line inside the first line. Make sure the width is equal.

How to Draw a Tree of Life

Another striking Celtic symbol is the tree of life, bold, beautiful, adorable, and unique. It has a few spiritual meanings, like other forms of Celtic patterns. Remember that Celts were highly religious people, and they had a way of linking their designs to religion. Learning how to draw the Celtic tree is fun since you can use it to embellish your projects. Good. So, I will now show you how to draw the tree with little or no assistance. Are you ready?

Materials Required

- Graph paper

- Pencil and eraser

- Pen or marker

- Ruler

- Compass

Instructions

Follow these simple steps to draw your own Celtic tree of life pattern.

Step 1: Begin With two curved sides of the tree to perfectly bend the upper curve twigs.

Step 2: Sketch the lower line and twigs.

Step 3: Insert two new center twigs.

Step 4: Move to the base, insert smaller twigs.

Step 5: Insert more smaller twigs.

Step 6: Insert ornamental shapes such as triangles.

Step 7: Insert decorations to the base.

Step 8: Indicate with a pointer and color with crayons.

How to Draw a Celtic Heart Knot

The heart symbolizes love. The Celtic heart is a gift of love. It is a design for someone you genuinely love and value—maybe your girlfriend or fiancé. Although the pattern is quite simple to draw, some quilters still have issues getting it right. Why? You're going to end up with something else if you miss a dot or a line. No worries. I will show you how to draw it perfectly, and you'll be producing a fantastic Celtic heart knot right there in your home. Here is how to design your Celtic heart knot.

Materials Required

- Graph paper

- Pencil and eraser

- Pen or marker

- Ruler

- Compass

Instructions

Follow these simple steps to draw your own Celtic heart knot.

Step 1: Just like the name indicates, draw out a heart and make sure you join both sides to form a diamond where the two ends meet at the top.

Step 2: Exploiting the lines for the diamond, design three linking lines. The three lines must curve a little bit.

Step 3: At the outer part of the heart drawn initially, draw another heart.

Step 4: At this time, when the two lines meet in the middle at the top, the line on the right goes straight down to the first heart, and the line on the left stops at the line on the right. Inside the heart itself, draw in the lines as shown to complete the lines that are already there to show them overlapping.

Step 5: Complete them by tracing the same line until you form three arrow-like points. Only the line on the right should overlap the heart in the center on each one of them.

Step 6: When you erase all the red lines, this is what you are left with. Make sure there are no breaks in the lines and that none of the lines are perfectly straight and you are totally finished.

How to Draw a Celtic Spiral

Celtic spiral is a charming design. It is bold and attractive. The Celtic spiral could be single, double, or triple, but all of them can beautify your quilts. Although there are variations on how you design the three spiral patterns, what I'll be sharing with you here will help you master Celtic spirals. Fine. Just pay keen attention to what we have here, and nothing will stop you from creating your Celtic spiral right there in your home.

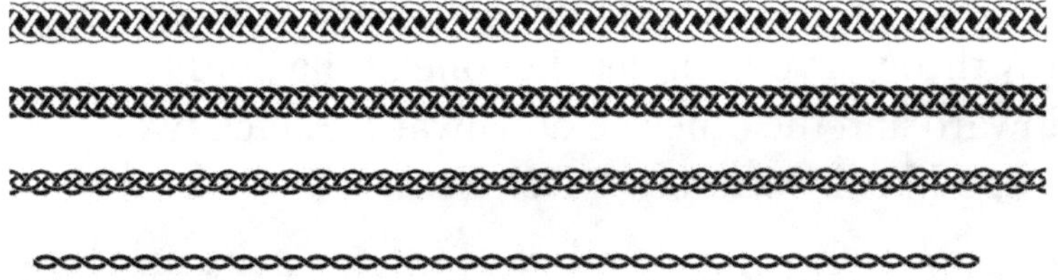

Materials Required

- Graph paper

- Pencil and eraser

- Pen or marker

- Ruler

Instructions

Follow these simple steps to design your own Celtic spiral.

Step 1: Begin the spiral with a circle with your compass placed one inch apart. Sketch another circle at the middle of the paper with your compass set at two inches apart.

Step 2: Sketch another circle with your compass set at three inches.

Note: you can increase your compass to four inches and even five inches, depending on the size of your drawing material.

Step 3: Sketch two lines across the circles all the way through your circles. Let one of the lines be upward and the other be downward. Sketch two "X" shape-like lines across the circles.

Step 4: Start to sketch a spiral. Each spiral should contain at least two or three curved angles. Draw an

"X" in each of these spirals to join the bottom left corner with the upper right.

Step 5: Finish the spiral. You should sketch eight lines that form spirals in each direction. These spirals should be both clockwise and anti-clockwise. Sketch the spiral again in a curve way. Then, spread the curved line into the center of the angle.

How to Draw Knotted Lines

With knotted lines, you can take your designs to higher heights. These lines are just too charming and beautiful to neglect. They can make your designs irresistible, and you'll love the outlook of your Celtic knot. Yet, creativity is required if you want to create a lovely and appealing knotted line. Don't worry. I will take you through the process of designing these lines.

Required Materials

- Graph paper

- Pencil and eraser

- Pen or marker

- Lightbox (optional)

- Contrasting colored pen or marker (optional)

- Unlined paper (optional)

Instructions

Follow these steps to draw your own knotted line with a graph.

Step 1: Sketch the Grid: First, sketch a zigzag grid with an even number of lines and columns—count two squares for each column and row—for example, 6 columns by 6 rows. Columns and rows can easily be counted using dots along the edges. Most times, your columns and your rows may not be the same. You can have 4 columns by 8 rows grid. Although there is no limit to the number of columns or rows you can have.

Step 2: Draw some Vertical and Horizontal Lines: Sketch few vertical and horizontal lines at any point you want. The line must contain an even number of squares and dots placed at the center of the line. Your creativity is needed here. Every line you created should lean towards your Celtic knot.

Step 3: Connect the Dots: Join all your dots with diagonal lines. Your vertical or horizontal lines drawn earlier should not be joined with any other lines. Complete the joining of the dots by sketching a curve between the dots near your vertical and horizontal lines. Note the interaction between the knot and the line drawn. It will allow you to get loops, waves, and corners in your knot.

Reduce the gaps by outlining over alternating dots as you trace the line of your knot. Find the meeting points in the lower-left corner. Connect the meeting point by tracing over that dot. Sketch over one, skip one, sketch over the next, and so on.

Step 4: Make it Fancy: You can make your knot look extra beautiful by widening or tightening up the gaps. This technique will make it look like a continuous rope. To make this, use a pen of different colors and draw lines on each side. Don't be too concerned about the gap of the point but make sure it is the same. Since you know the secret, I believe you can configure your own Celtic knot now and understand the size of all types of knots.

Uses of the Celtic Knot Design

The uses of Celtic knot designs are many. Let start by looking at creative art, jewelry, clothing, and home decoration. You will understand that Celtic knot designs are integrated into all of these areas. This alone can make wedding rings and other jewelry look beautiful.

Celtic knot designs are commonly imprinted or decorated into leather to make pocketbooks, wallets, and clothing materials. The art of inscription is enabled heavily by the use of Celtic knot designs. It is also employed alongside the sides of the page and as initial letters of paragraphs. It can sometimes even show up in the middle of sentences to emphasize a point or an idea. Learning to design and draw Celtic knots can add a new dimension to whatever art form you choose.

Some knots can be used for decorative purposes, while others are used for deeper purposes with in-depth meaning.

Some Celtic families used to have their own knot for refrain and entertainment, this allowed them to customize it easily, and it is known to the family alone. Of course, there were also knots in Celtic that carry the same meaning and symbol for everyone. This includes the spiral knot or the sailor's knot.

The spread of Christianity made it forbidden for Celts and other heathens to practice their faith. The Celts found a way around this by hiding small Celtic elements in their stories. They also integrated the knots in Christian artwork.

Countless numbers of knots can also be found on gravestones, churches, and manuscripts, where these Celtic knots were used to beautify letters. In crosses, the knotwork is also used in addition to Biblical stories. For example, the Celtic cross is made with ornamentation of Celtic knots.

Drawing Celtic Knot Designs

To make use of Celtic knot designs, you must be able to sketch them as decorations. There are a few methods that can help you improve your knowledge on this.

Graph Paper Method

This may require you to use graph paper and Ink for the sketching. This is for the Beginners. Sketching by hand is seen as time-consuming, but the best way to draw Celtic knots by some purists. You will sketch a rectangle on the graph paper, which contains an odd number of angles in both length and width. All odd numbers are allowed. Then input dots to each corner of the rectangle and every other square on each side.

Make use of multiple colored pencils, sketch a dot on the next line inside your original rectangle. Avoid sketching the second of dots at the corners. When you have finished putting the rectangle of dots inside the original rectangle, you will draw slanting lines from the inside dot to the other inside dot, beginning with the top left.

Then go to the top right and draw diagonal lines again from inside dot to inside dot. It helps to use a ruler during this step to keep your guidelines perfectly straight. When you have finished connecting the inside dots going both directions, you will have created a grid that can be used to create your Celtic knot design. By using curving lines and straight lines in a balanced fashion on the grid, you can create many beautiful and unique Celtic knots.

Computer-Drawn Celtic Knot Designs

Most people are not interested in the old way of drawing Celtic knot designs. There are several other ways to use computer programs to sketch Celtic knot designs. Computer programs, such as Adobe Illustrator, allow you to test and try out with color quickly and easily. Computer programs will enable you to copy a design section and repeat it as often as you would like. This process hastens the job and makes it look neat and simple. This style also enables you to create big, complex, and sophisticated Celtic knot designs quickly. Other drafting programs, such as AutoCAD, can be used to design the knotwork and do Celtic jewelry mockups.

Celtic knot designs are attractive and gorgeous. They contain a rich cultural and historical background and legacy. Celtic knot designs are symbolic and carry meaning inside meaning and many complex ideas. Knowing how to draw Celtic knot designs manually or through computer system programs may look frightening or discouraging. Still, it can be done by anyone interested and who wants to put effort into doing it. The result of that effort will be a whole new design aspect to add to your art or craft. Celtic knots can add a unique flair to jewelry, leather, cloth, calligraphy, or even tattoo designs.

Chapter Summary

- Braids, twists, and knotted lines are used to beautify quilts.

- The Celtic cross is used to design pendants, jewelries, and rings.

In the next chapter, you will learn about Celtic patterns.

Chapter Four:
Celtic Patterns

Celtic patterns are highly intricate knots and graphical images of knots that serve mainly as aesthetics and decoration, originating from Celtic art. These knots are popular because of how widely used and represented in Christian monuments and manuscripts. Examples of these are found in the Book of Kells, the Lindisfarne Gospels, and the 8th- century St. Teilo Gospels.

Most Celtic patterns are endless knots and appear in various varieties of basket weave knots.

How to Draw a Line and Border Patterns

Drawing a line and border pattern is relatively easy, but you need to pay attention when drawing your grid and pattern so that it comes out correctly. Just follow these simple steps to design your own line and border pattern.

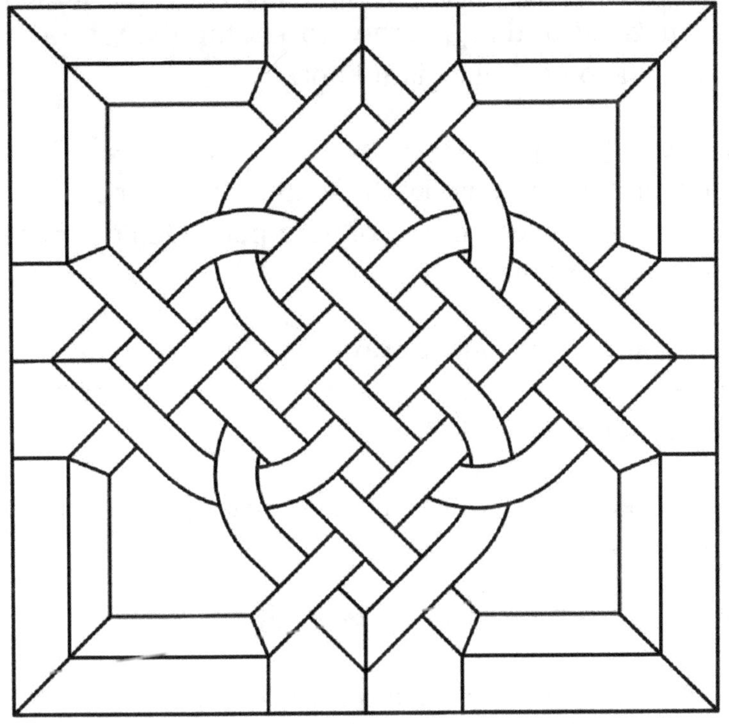

Step 1: As a beginner, use a grid. It is best to use a big grid because it makes drawing the pattern easier.

Step 2: Put the grid under your drawing paper and trace the grid to create a border. A rectangle is better and more comfortable.

Step 3: Start drawing your squares inside the grid and squares around from the four corners of the grid and work your way towards the center of the paper.

Step 4: Continue drawing under, over, and under alternatively and repeat the process for about 500 times till you get one giant knot.

Step 5: Try to keep your lines symmetrical. Draw your lines again to make them appear bolder and straighter. You can use a coloring pencil to add more color to your knot.

Step 6: You could always switch styles by making more or fewer corners, make a double border with a frame, add colors, circles, etc.

The goal is to have fun while creating your line and border pattern.

How to Make a Corner Pattern

A corner pattern can aid the aesthetics of your Celtic knot. It is beautiful if it is well-crafted. Some designers often complain that the corner pattern is a bit complex, but you have nothing to worry about. Here, I will teach you how to create a corner pattern in the comfort of your home.

Required Materials

- Graph paper

- Colored pencils

- Marker

- An eraser

Instructions

Follow these simple steps to design your corner pattern.

Step 1: Place your basic units in a string and connect each unit with curves.

Step 2: Use a simple or complex corner unit to connect your unit seamlessly.

Step 3: End the string you made with an end unit using half your string's width.

Step 4: Shade your units with a pencil to add shadows to overlapped bands. Keep the width of your bands equal.

Step 5: Connect the bands that face the outside border.

Step 6: Start with forming basic units. Connect The tops and bottoms of each unit with curves. Connect the middle ends with straight lines. Ensure the bands that start on top - go under, the bands that begin below - go above.

Step 7: Create a knot in each corner to tangle your bands.

Step 8: Turn one of your bands into a curve that ends on the axis. Your curve can take any shape.

Step 9: Your outside curve should be the same as the first one and go through the same key point on the axis.

Step 10: Extend the other band into a different curve, add width, and ensure they end on the same axis.

Step 11: Interweave all line units you've drawn and erase every part that appears overlapped.

Step 12: Erase all pencil marks and use a marker to outline.

Step 13: Shade your unit when you are done to smooth, blend, and create a realistic drop shadow effect.

How to Draw Celtic Circles and Squares

Celtic circles and squares can make your Celtic knotwork beautiful and charming. Just design these circles and squares with creativity, and you'll love the final output. How do I create my Celtic circles or squares? No worries. Here is how.

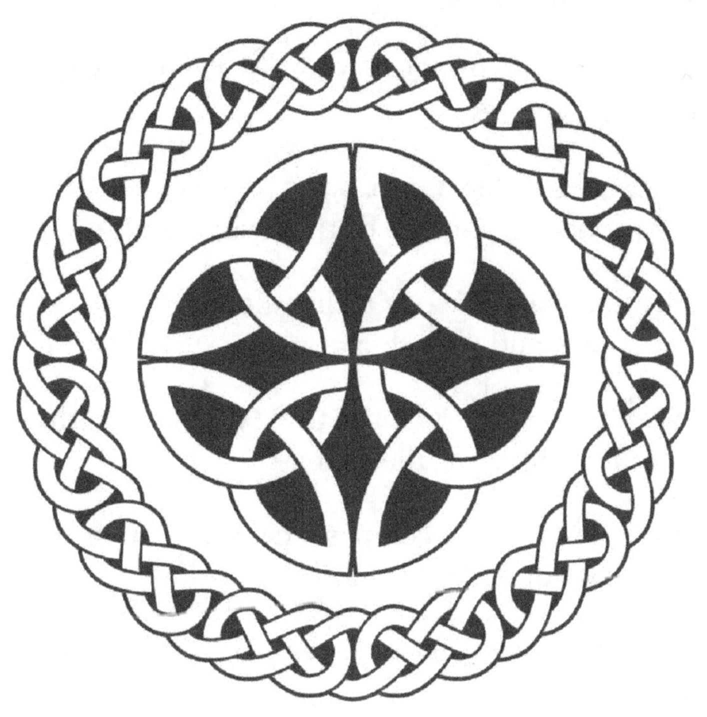

Required Materials

- Graph paper

- Compass

- Colored pencils

- An eraser

- Compass and protractor

Instructions

Follow these simple steps to create your own Celtic circles and squares.

Step 1: Divide your drawing paper into half and pick a particular point to be the circle's center.

Step 2: Measure two inches along the radius from the midpoint and make a mark.

Step 3: Make 1/4 inches three times apart that are moving back towards the center.

Step 4: Use your compass to set a point in the midpoint, to outside the mark.

Step 5: Draw your circle, keeping the point of the compass at the midpoint.

Step 6: Draw four such circles with the largest being 4" in diameter, the next being 3 1/2, 3, and 2 1/2, respectively.

Step 7: Use a protractor to line the 0 marks upon your center line and do the same on your midpoint center.

Step 8: Make little tick marks every 10 degrees. Ten degrees is about the same size as the 1/4" of a standard graph sheet.

Step 9: Use a ruler to draw in guidelines on both sides of the circle you've drawn. I know this is a lot, but you'll get the perfect Celtic Circle and square. Let's continue the process.

Step 10: Start drawing in the "bones" of the braid you've made.

Step 11: Draw in your curves & start the weaving pattern. Make sure you erase the bones before making your curves. Remember, your braid won't be a band of interlace when they connect if the number of curves on the outside edge can be equally divided by three.

Step 12: Draw two relatively long parallel lines that are 1/2 inches apart and make tic marks on the top and bottom every two inches.

Step 13: Draw in your top and bottom curves, ensuring they are centered between the tic marks and letting the right-hand side cross over the space onto the next arc as they will form the outer edge of your bands.

Step 14: Next, draw in the inner edge of your bands from the top and extend your lines a bit more to ensure that the inner edge is aligned to form the lower curved outer edge and create an "over" portion of the twist.

Step 15: Complete the lower curves while trying to keep the width of your bands even.

Don't worry if your first trial looks very messy. You've got an eraser, and you can always erase rough edges and pencil marks. Practice makes perfect. Once you keep practicing, your circle and square pattern will appear less messy.

Viking Animals

Hundreds of Viking jewelry items with various symbols are sold across different jewelry stores all over the world. Why are these Viking jewels famous? You may ask. There is no definite meaning and origin of these Viking symbols since most are anthropological, historical, and archaeological guesses. However, it is still necessary to understand the Viking symbols' true source, background, and meaning.

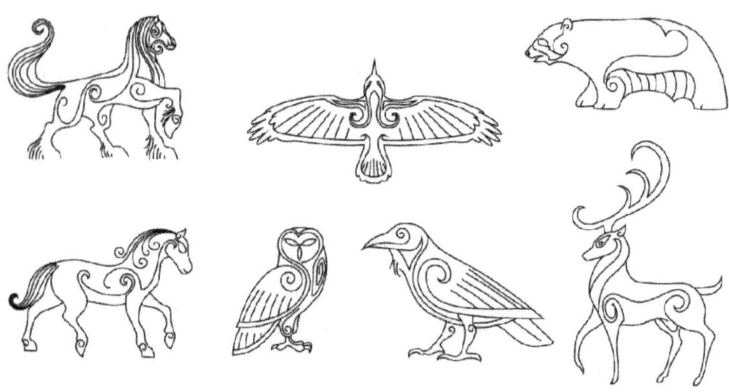

The Norse used these iconic Viking images and symbols during the Viking era. A high percentage of Modern Icelandic people have been argued to be direct descendants of Viking ancestors. A lot of these symbols such as the well-known Helm of Awe

(Icelandic: Ægishjálmur, Old Norse Œgishjalmr) and the Viking Compass (Icelandic: Vegvísir, for "signpost" or "Wayfinder") were said to have been found in ancient Icelandic books from the 16th century.

These books were a collection of old magical runes passed from one generation to another. However, some other Viking symbols have no proof of originating from the Viking era. An example is the Troll Cross, and the true origin of these symbols remains uncertain. At the end of the Viking era, Vikings were already beginning to blend with the other cultures they settled in. Many of the last few generations of these Vikings were often the children of Celtic, Slavic, English parents.

How to Draw a Viking Animal

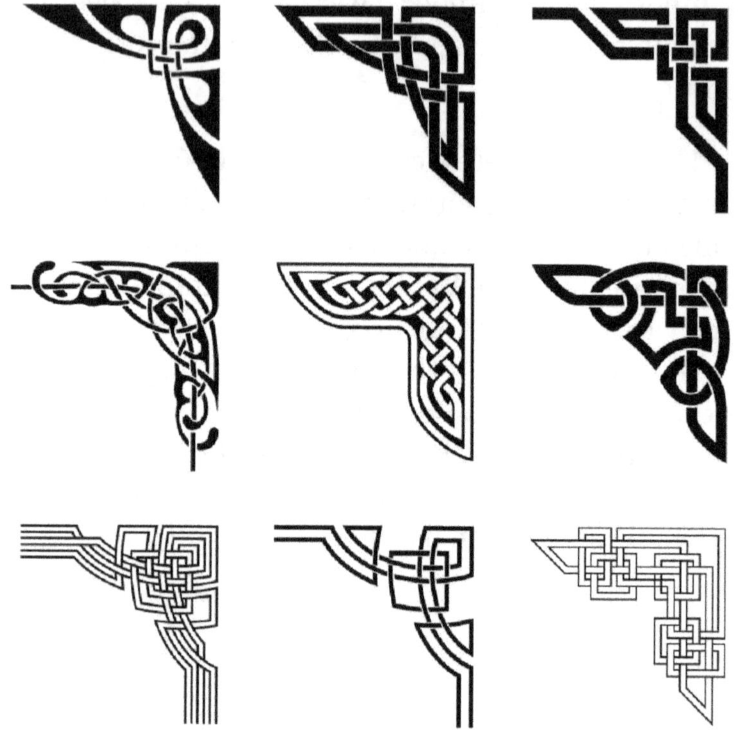

Step 1: Let's start by using a large oval shape to create the head of your Viking animal.

Step 2: Next, draw in a thin rectangle to represent the body, and you can also make the pants in the same pattern.

Step 3: Work repeatedly on this Viking animal by sketching the arms and the legs. No fingers are needed, so draw a simple circle to replace the fingers and shoes.

Step 4: Create the eyes and the pupils from large circles. Then draw smaller circular shapes to form the ears. The helmet is made using a rectangle with rounded corners while you create the horns from curved lines.

Step 5: Draw a few oval shapes to form the pupils while drawing a line representing the nose and mouth. Go ahead and draw a large beard around the mouth and some hair below the head.

Step 6: complete your Viking animal by adding a broad belt of the shirt and a pointed sword on the right hand of your drawn Viking animal.

Step 7: Add colors to make your Viking animal more aesthetic.

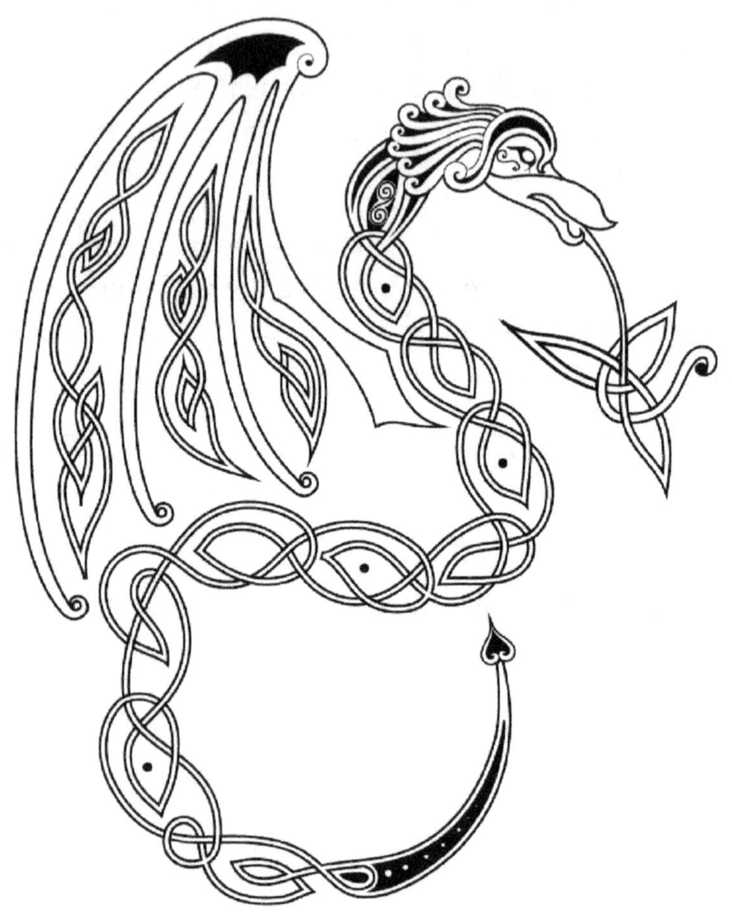

Celtic Religious Symbols and Their Meanings

Celtic symbols and signs have held incredible power for the ancient Celts in every way of life since a long time ago.

These ancient Celtic communities used Celtic symbols and images for worship, and they firmly believed in the power these symbols wielded. Now all of these have become a part of the Irish heritage and identity. Some of these Celtic symbols and their meaning includes:

- The Awen: The word 'Awen' first appeared in the 9th-century book titled "HistoriaBrittonum," which means inspiration or essence.

People attribute various meanings to the Celtic Awen symbol. One such interpretation is that the Awen represents the harmony of both opposites of the universe.

For instance, the two outer rays represent masculine and feminine energy, while the ray in the middle represents the balance between them.

- St. Brigid's Cross: St. Brigid's Cross is believed to be a Christian symbol, but ancient Irish Celtic Mythology associated Brigid's Cross with a life-giving goddess, known as Brigid of the Tuatha de Danann. When Christians came to settle in Ireland, the goddess became anglicized to St Brigid of Kildare. Most of her attributes, especially her association with fire, were transferred to the latter.

The cross is woven from rushes and straws and is used during the feast of Imbolc to signify the beginning of spring.

- Celtic Cross: Just like with the Brigid's Cross, many people associate the Celtic Cross with Christianity, although studies seem to suggest that this symbol predates Christianity by thousands of years.

The symbol has appeared in many ancient cultures, and according to one theory, the Celtic Cross represents the four cardinal directions of the earth. Another theory posits that the Celtic Cross represents the four essential elements, which are Earth, Air, Water, and fire.

The Celtic Cross has powerful representations and meanings that are a perfect reflection of the Celts' hopes and ambitions. While the Christians believe the Celtic Cross is undoubtedly a Christian symbol, research has proven otherwise as it has its roots in ancient pagan beliefs.

- The Green Man: The Green Man is represented in many cultures as the head of human-made foliage. This image is often seen in many buildings and structures in Ireland and even Britain. People believe the Green Man is a symbol of rebirth and the co-dependence and interconnectedness between nature and man.

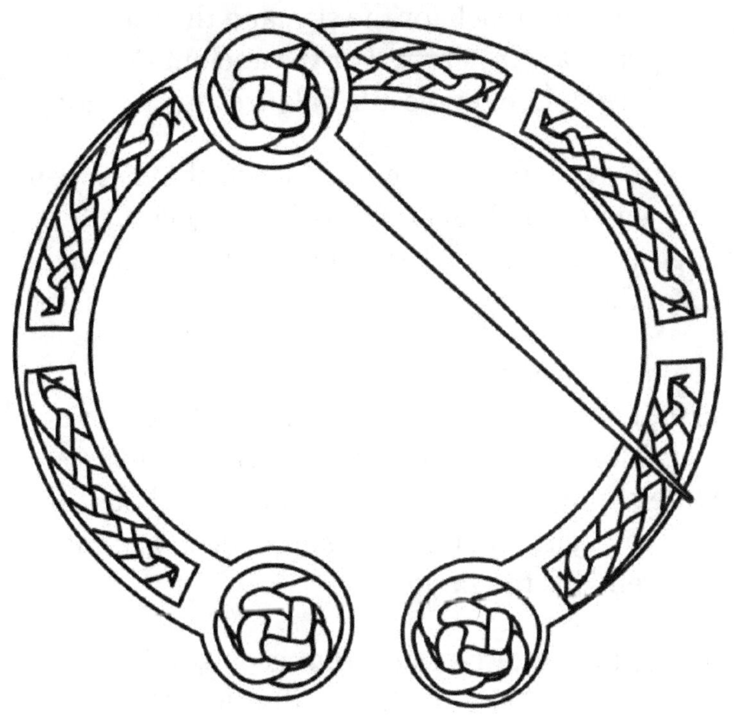

The Green man symbolizes the lushness of vegetation and also the arrival of spring and summer. Christian churches have also carved the Green man in their art, such as the Seven Green Men of Nicosia in Cyprus, a series of green men carved in the 29th century onto the facade of St Nicholas Church in Nicosia.

- The Tree of Life: The Celtic Tree of Life, also known as 'CrannBethadh' in Irish, are intricately interwoven branches and roots often associated with the Druids. It is a potent and earthy Celtic symbol. In representations, the branches reach for the sky, and the roots permeate the earth. For the ancient Celts, the Tree of Life represents balance and harmony.

It also symbolizes the close relationship between heaven and earth. It also stands for longevity, strength, and wisdom. The Celts also believed that the spirit of their dead ancestors lived in these trees.

They believed that these trees also symbolize rebirth (as they witnessed the trees shed old leaves during fall and grow new ones in spring), which made the tree highly revered. The unique thing about this symmetric Celtic is that when spun, its appearance always remains the same.

- Dara knot: The Dara Knot is one of the most popular Celtic symbols is the Dara Celtic Knot. This symbol is an interwoven design. It got its name from the Irish word 'Doire,' which means "oak tree." The Dara Knot symbol represents an ancient oak tree's root system and is made of intertwined lines with no beginning or end, which is common among Celtic Knot symbols.

There are several designs for the Dara Celtic Knot. However, all versions and modifications are centered on the oak tree's common theme and its roots. Ancient Celts and Druids revered nature, particularly old oak trees, and considered them sacred. They often saw the oak tree as a symbol of strength, power, wisdom, and endurance; hence the Dara Knot symbol represents inner strength, endurance, power, and wisdom.

Chapter Summary

- Celtic patterns are used for aesthetics and decorations.

- Celtic knots are widely used and represented in Christian monuments.

Were you able to create your own Celtic pattern?

In the next chapter, you will learn a few layout ideas.

Chapter Five: Layout Ideas

The Celtic layout can make or mar a Celtic art design. To a large extent, the layout determines the aesthetics of the knotwork. Remember that Celtic knot patterns are the combination of borders, corners, interlocking knots, and the designer's layout skills will determine how these things turn out. These borders, corners, and interlocking knots constitute the areas of concern when Celtic layout ideas are concerned.

Little wonder, designers, especially beginners in Celtic artwork, are eager to understand the fundamentals of Celtic borders, corners, interlocking knots, and all forms of dots and lines and how to use them to create amazing Celtic designs. This chapter will teach you two distinct methods of crafting unique and appealing layouts for your Celtic creations; tricks on how to create your own square, rectangle, or circular border, and some other incredible designs.

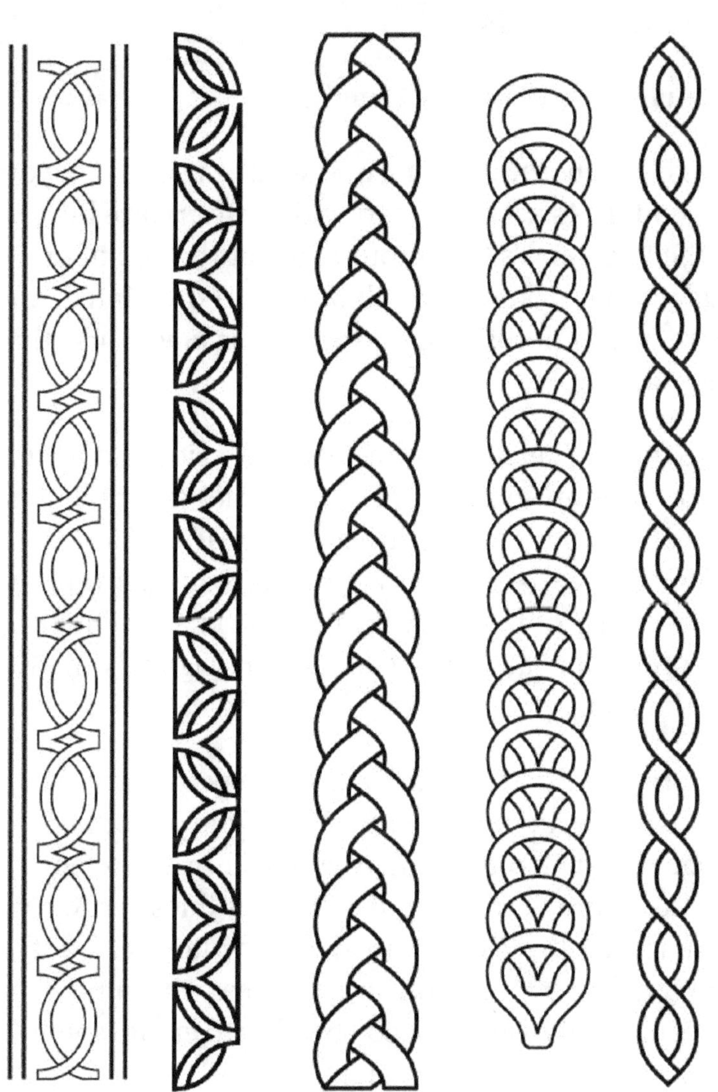

Layout Methods

Interlacing Without Erasing

There's nothing to erase when one uses this layout method. Dots used in creating the pattern are buried in the knotwork's background. So, at the end of the design, the background will be carved or painted, and there will be nothing to erase. Here is how to use this method.

Step 1: Sketch a few rectangular grids of dots. Fill up the section you want to add your knotwork but make sure that the dots are evenly spaced. To calculate the distance between dots, consider the width of the ribbons of your knotwork. Add a dot to the middle of each square to form a diagonal dot grid for the knotwork project.

Step 2: Add the breaks. Use breaks to vary the loop of your knotwork, or use the same pattern all through. The knotwork may run over lines, except the breaks. A break can join two or more lines vertically or horizontally. While a break could intersect a dot, one break must not cross another one within the design. Breaks can be used stylishly to create some striking effects in Celtic knotwork.

Step 3: Weave the ribbon. Locate the open area next to the break, and start the weaving from there. To indicate the start of the ribbon, sketch two diagonal lines in the center of two dots. Sketch two more diagonal lines opposite the first set and expand the drawing a bit to create a regular knotwork weaving pattern.

Step 4: Curve the breaks, but note that your ribbon must not cross your break. While your ribbon takes a diagonal slant, the breaks could be horizontal or vertical. So, just before you hit the break lines, find a way to bend your ribbon.

You don't need to create an initial layout before you can use this method. With the technique, all you need to put in place are the grids. Use this layout method to design great and amazing projects to amuse your friends and loved ones.

Centerline Knotwork

Most people prefer the first layout method. Why? They believe that the centerline knotwork is too complex to master. True, it is an ancient method of layout since it was used in the Book of Kells. With this method, you'll need to sketch more lines than expected and also erase some. Still, this layout method shares some similarities with the previous one. Here, I will show you the processes, and if it works perfectly for you, you can use it to design your knotwork layout.

Step 1: Sketch a few rectangular grids of dots. Yes, the first process is similar to that of the previous one. But, in this case, the number of dots in a direction should be odd. To make this happen, divide the odds in the direction by two, and you'll know if what you have is odd or not. Next, add a dot in the center of each square.

Step 2: Add the breaks. Control the ribbon with the break, just like you did with the first method. Still, you don't have to connect the dots. Center the break on the dots. Feel free to join the breaks if that will aid the aesthetics of your knotwork. Just remember that breaks cannot hit the dots directly. All you can use them to do is intersect two or more dots.

Step 3: Sketch the middle line. Connect your diagonal dots to create the ribbon's centerline. Follow this line until you need to avoid hitting the break. So, find a way to bend the middle line, but you can connect it with the nearest dot. Run the middle line till you get to where you initiated the drawing. Should you miss any dots, feel free to connect the dots again or initiate the process of sketching another centerline. So, as it stands, you'll have more drawings to sketch and more lines to erase.

Again, the centerline knotwork method is time-consuming. You'll have to create many centrelines and tilt them to your desired position to create your favorite pattern. Still, if you used a single line, you can easily modify your ribbon's movement just by altering your breaks. There's no way you can use the previous method to achieve this.

Step 4: Sketch the highway. Always consider your centerline as the road or pathway for your knotwork layout. Simply sketch the edges of the layout beside the centerline if you want the whole process to be very easy. Once this is done, you'll discover that your ribbon has three major lines— a center edge and two outer edges.

Step 5: Weave the ribbon. Identify two intersection points in the design. Consider them as the crossing points of the pathway of your knotwork. Use a few lines to bridge the two roads.

Step 6: Erase the centerline. Initially, I told you that this layout method uses lots of centerlines, and you'll need to erase a few ones after the whole design is done. So, take your time to erase the excess centerlines, one after the other.

Feel free to try these two layout methods to know the one that works best for you. The first method is considerably easier to use than the second one. Just know that the second layout method often leads to a more beautiful layout design.

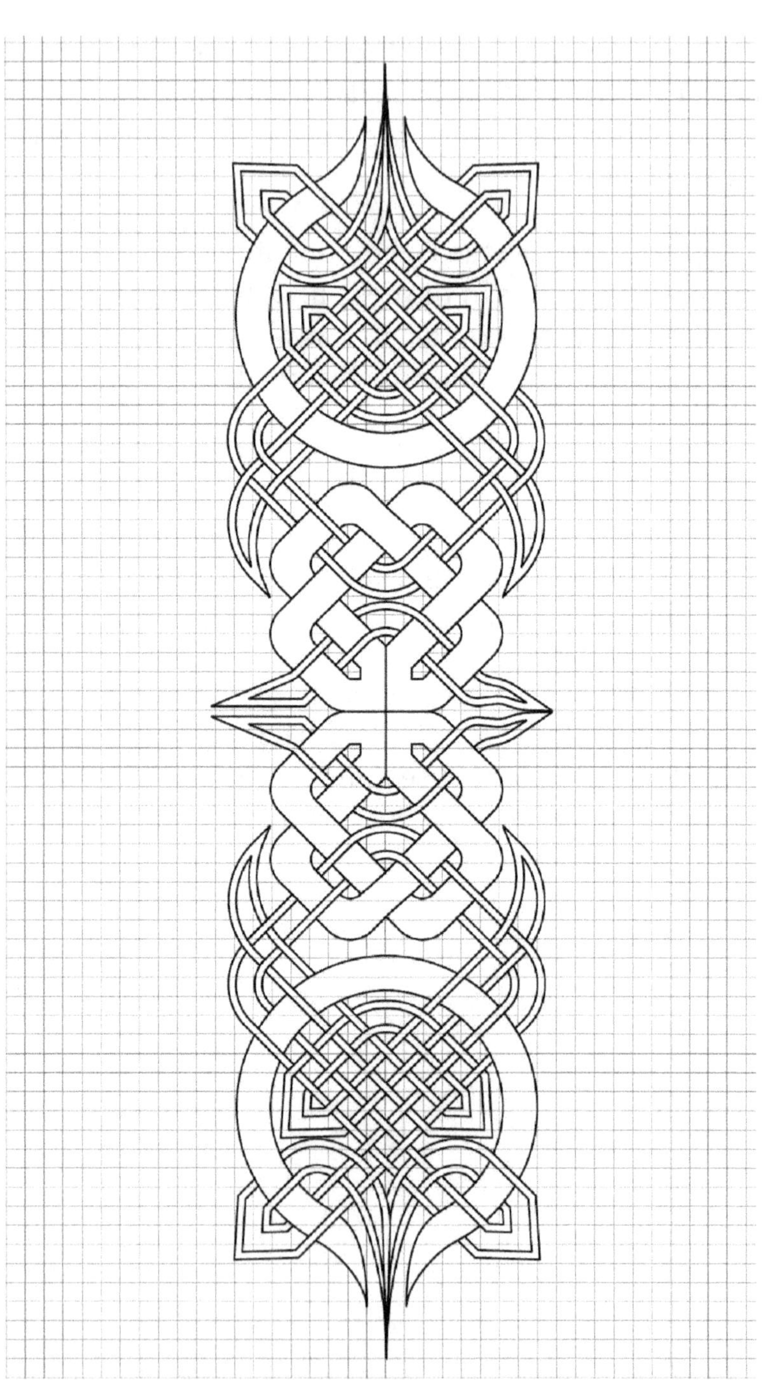

How to Create a Circular Border

A circular border is fair and fitting, but some people believe it is a bit complicated. Some say a circular border is easier than drawing straight lines. Fine. It depends on which one works best for you and how easy it is for you to create them. Still, both circular borders and straight lines can have a substantial visual impact on your Celtic knot. Here is how to design a circular border.

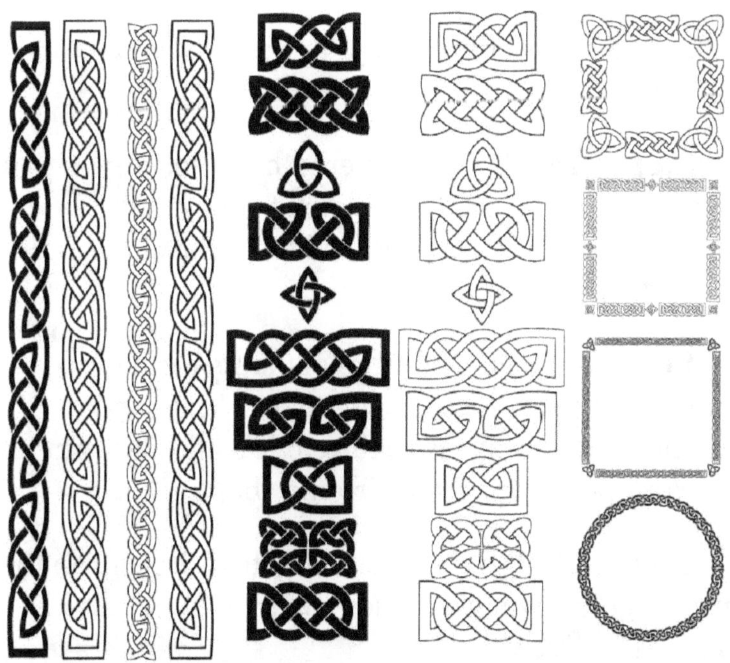

Required Materials

- Graph paper

- Colored pencils

- Compass and protractor

- An eraser

- Ruler

Instructions

Follow these simple steps to design your circular border.

Step 1: Divide your paper in half. Decide the point you intend to use as the middle of your circle. Measure 2 inches from the middle of the circle and mark the point.

Step 2: Sketch 3 additional marks from the middle of the circle, but keep them 1/4" apart. Position your compass to the circle's middle point and use your pencil to create a round shape.

Step 3: Sketch the circle. Create a circle from the middle point. Draw 4 circles— 4", 3 1/2", 3", and 2 1/2" respectively.

Step 4: Sketch your curves around the circle and add your weave pattern.

Step 5: Erase rough lines. Color your design. Feel free to use the color you want. Just make sure that you balance your color.

How to Design a Celtic Knot with a Rectangle Border

Borders aid the aesthetics of Celtic knots. They ensure that the designed knot looks attractive and appealing. Again, you can vary the rectangles, circles, and squares to create the knot you truly want. Good. Here is how to create a Celtic knot with a rectangle border.

Required Materials

- Grainy or graph paper

- Colored pencils

- An eraser

Instructions

Follow these simple steps to design a Celtic knot with a rectangle border.

Step 1: Use a grid to design the border. Just make sure that the grid is big, or you'll have issues perfecting this stage. Lay the grid on a flat surface and put the paper on it. Use your pencil to trace the grid to design your rectangle border.

Step 2: Finish the pattern. Stylishly work on the corners and glide your hand to the center of the knot. Here, you'll sketch two squares— one within the grid and the other one on the edges of the grid square. Add a few curves when you're connecting the squares if you want to make the design a little fancy. Sure, creativity is desirable here.

Step 3: Run the line over the grid a few times. Take your time here because you'll be going to run the line a couple of times again. Just make sure you get the shape you admire.

Step 4: Finish the design. Straighten and thicken the lines to make them look attractive and appealing. Feel free to color the design.

Creativity is key. Again, rather than creating four or five borders, stick to two. Create a frame and color the design. Use your favorite color.

Chapter Summary

- Celtic layout can be used to determine and aid the aesthetics of the Celtic knotwork.

- Borders, corners, and interlocking knots are used to create celtic layout.

In the next chapter, you will learn how to enhance your Celtic pattern with color.

Chapter Six:
A Guide to Enhancing Your Work with Color

Patterns are everywhere, and we must have seen and purchased different items with highly intricate colors and patterns. They are mostly aesthetic and best for decorations. However, you have to know how to create these patterns, especially as a designer. This is important because patterns invoke movement, aids color harmony, create visual texture, and make your work visually appealing.

What if I'm not into patterns? That is not a problem as many people feel that way until they create a pattern themselves. Creating a pattern can be quite tricky, especially for beginners, but you will become a professional at creating beautiful patterns with time. One predominant question here is this: How do you mix colors and patterns?

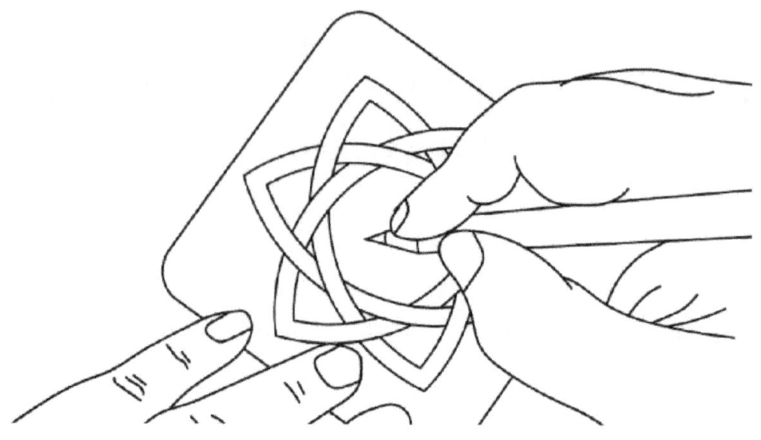

Know Your Colors

To create a perfect mix of colors and patterns, you have to outline your color scheme. You have to understand the 60-30-10 color rule. This means you have to choose three colors: the primary, secondary, and accent color in the 60:30:10 ratio, respectively. This will help you know which colors complement each other and how to incorporate these colors effectively.

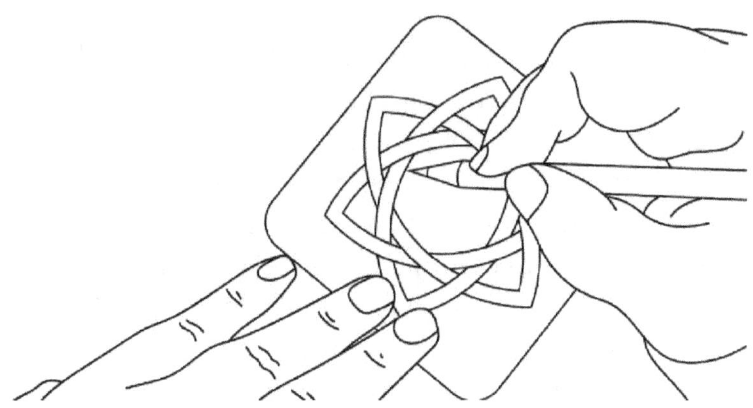

Your primary color (60%) is the most extensive color element and is often a neutral one. It is the color that anchors how the whole space would turn out. The secondary color (30%) is usually different from the primary color and creates a huge contrast to create a harmonious balance. Lastly, your accent color (10%) is mainly used for accessories and creates a huge visual impact.

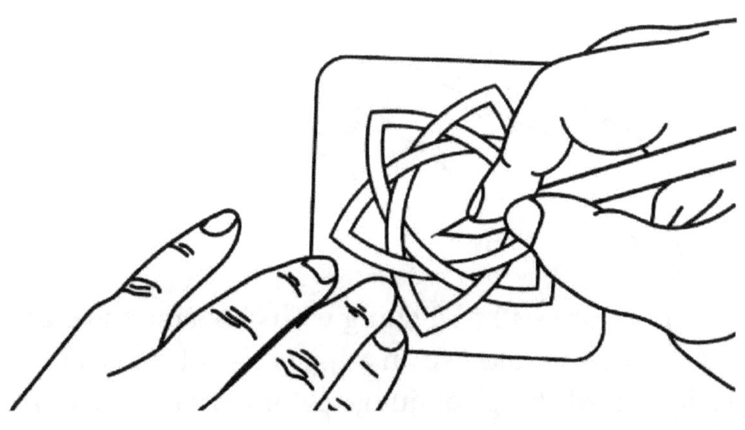

Know How to Balance the Color Temperature

Colors have temperatures, and these can either be warm or cool. Warm colors are red, yellow, and orange, while cool colors are blue, green, and violet. When choosing the right colors for mixing, choose both warm and cool to create a harmonious balance. Using only warm colors can create a visually stuffy effect, and using only cool makes your art appear visually chilly. However, a combination of both will make your art seem nice and appealing.

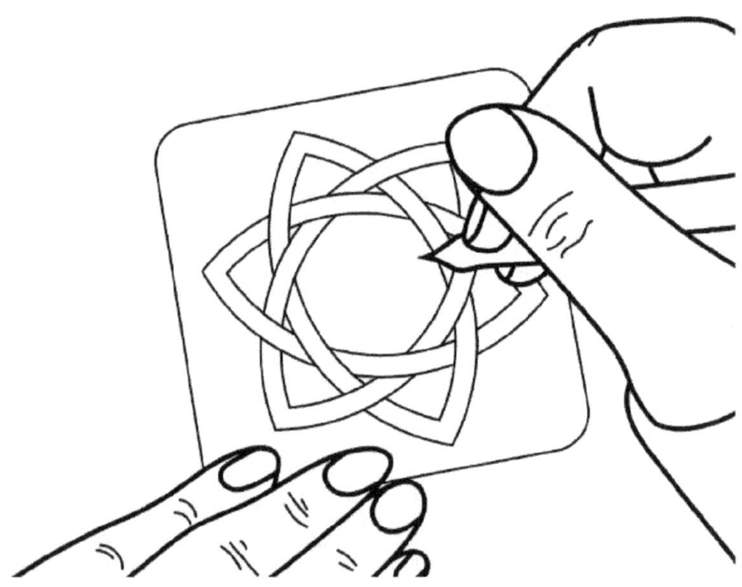

Use a Color Wheel

If you are still struggling with choosing the right colors, you should use an adjustable color wheel. Color wheels help you judge color undertones more accurately and also assist you in creating harmonious color combinations. They also help you know the difference between warm and cool colors.

You can use a color wheel to create vibrant color combinations as they help indicate what color pairings are harmonious. For example, all complementary colors are best for contrasting an accent, primary or secondary color. Also, a Triad (split complementary color) is best for selecting a 3-color limited pattern, while the Tetrad is used to choose an additional accent color for your art.

Gradient Colors Weaving with Rya Knots: Weaving Color

This topic is geared at teaching you how to weave a gradient color effect along with your soumak and plain weave, rya knots, and yarn. The main reason this is done is to create movement and depth in weaving and enhance the visuals.

Learning this technique is also great for creating transitions between textures of different yarns. All you have to do is add both colors alternatively to achieve this.

How to Weave Gradient Colors with Rya Knots

Rya knots are created with one, two, or more strands of yarn. When you see more colors on your Rya knot, it increases the color intensity of the knot. To weave gradient colors with Rya knots, there is a process of layering you have to follow.

Instructions

1. Get two yarns that are of different colors.

2. Pick two strands from each yarn.

3. Start weaving your first row with color.

4. Weave the second row with color 2.

5. Weave the first row again with color 1 and 2.

6. Weave the second row with color 1.

7. Start again by weaving the first row with color 1 and color 2.

Weave the second row with color 1 and color 2.

Repeat the process by weaving the first row with color 1.

Start the second row with just one strand of color 2.

Then create a third row with two strands of color 1.

There is another method to create a gradient color with Rya knots. The instructions are below:

Step 1: Weave a few rows of plain weave to serve as your base.

Step 2: Weave two or three rows of your Rya knot using color one.

Step 3: Always secure your knot after weaving two or three rows.

Step 4: After weaving a substantial amount of rows, use color two.

Step 5: Repeat the process alternatively depending on your desired outcome

Step 6: Make sure your knot has a combination of both colors, and always remember to secure your knots after weaving two to four rows.

Step 7: Introduce the third color you want to use.

Step 8: Repeat the process from step 6 to 1 in reverse order.

5 Simple Tips to Achieve Color Harmony In Your Oil Painting

What do you understand by the term 'Color Harmony'? The word itself is self-explanatory. Still, it has to do with combining colors in a way that is harmonious to the eyes. Most artists refer to it as the 'magical glue' connecting all elements of your painting together. When your colors lack harmony, even when you have a perfect idea, strong composition, and a powerful paint composition, you will still likely end up creating a painting that holds no appeal to the eyes that view them.

Colors are an essential part of our lives, and almost everything we see has color and is highlighted by the lighting conditions of the atmosphere. Natural colors often appear harmonious, and there is often a strong need to replicate these on your canvas. There are many rules as to how to achieve such harmony for complementary or analogous colors. You can reach the best color harmony when painting; only if you understand and practice the following tips, which we shall be discussing below.

1. Always start your painting with ground color. Doing this makes your work easier as you don't have to fill up every gap on your canvas. The ground color allows you to create a stable atmosphere that makes it easy to harmonize your painting. Your ground color can vary depending on what you want to paint.

2. Learn to use a limited palette. Buying every color feels good but using fewer colors, especially when mixing, has many benefits. Using too many colors can create an overall chaotic and disorganized effect. A limited palette makes it easier to mix, and it helps enhance color harmony.

3. One tricky tip to creating color harmony on your piece is to use different colors with the same painting brush. That is, don't wipe your brushes. When you do this, you'll discover that although you used varying shades, they appear harmonious and share the same pigment.

4. Always add colors across your canvas for better blending and ensure that no area is untouched, which aids and adds to your piece's visuals. This helps to harmonize the colors and link all elements together.

5. Glazing your painting is a great way to achieve color harmony. Glaze your artwork to achieve a specific mood and reduce the intensity of the colors on the canvas. To add your glaze, use a retouching varnish or painting medium along with little paint to avoid cracks.

10 Oil Painting Techniques to Transform Your Artwork

Paintings are beautiful works of art, and as a painter, it is fun to paint lovely images and your imaginations on a canvas. However, you can go from painting simple crafts to creating a masterpiece using oil painting techniques.

Using the oil painting technique can be quite tricky as a beginner, and a mistake can ruin the result you are aiming for. Although there are several practical painting techniques to improve your painting art, it is still crucial that you know how you can also use oil painting techniques to help boost your painting skill and appearance.

If you want to give your art a boost with these professional oil painting techniques, you must note the ten fundamental tips for using the oil painting techniques available.

Hold Your Paint Brush Correctly

Many artists don't know this, but the way you handle your brush when painting, to some extent, determines how accurate your strokes will appear. Always hold your paintbrush at the end to gain maximum control of your strokes while painting. As an artist, it is essential to know how to handle your paintbrush to achieve fluidity and sensitivity when creating your strokes. You have to hold your paintbrush as far back as you can to achieve this.

As a beginner who is still learning to paint, this may prove a bit uncomfortable, but with constant practice, you will discover that it gives you some measure of control as you can paint with your whole arm, rather than using just your wrist, which gets tiring after a while.

Master Your Brush Orientation

Knowing your brush orientation is a great way to produce professional paintings. You don't always have to use only the flat side of your brush, as every paintbrush has two orientations and sides. Learn to use every angle of your brush as you get to create sharper lines, strokes, and control how these appear on your canvas. Once you understand this, you will discover that you become faster and more versatile when painting.

Vary Your Pressure

The pressure you apply when painting, especially when creating your lines and strokes, determines if that painting will come out perfect or messy. Avoid using a lot of pressure when handling your paintbrush, as the less pressure you apply, the better the texture of the painting. There are different types of strokes, and these are the Light, Medium, and Heavy strokes. Get acquainted with these strokes and the right pressure to apply to create each of them and achieve the desired effect.

Vary your pressure appropriately to ensure that they match your strokes for an overall aesthetic effect as the more massive your pressure, the more your paints will create ridges along the sides of your brushstrokes.

Harness the Power of the Painting Medium

As an artist, the best way to control paint is to use a painting medium. The painting medium can help modify your paints in ways you can't imagine. A painting medium is a mixture of solvent and oil that is used to control your paint. When you add a lot of painting medium to your regular paint, it becomes transparent and flat. Meanwhile, adding just a little painting medium makes your paint thicker, giving it a mayonnaise-like effect.

Keep Your Color Pure

Owning different paint brushes is essential. Keeping them clean is also another important task. Using a messy paint brush can mess up the color you want to use for a particular painting. Therefore, you have to keep your brushes clean after every painting session to ensure that they preserve the intensity of the colors you want to use for a new painting.

Use Two-Color Mixtures If You Can.

One trick to achieving a vibrant painting is to use as little color mix as possible. Using too many color mix can make your artwork appear dull and less intense. Instead, choose only two colors and mix them with white. You'll discover that your painting comes out better, and you become more efficient at selecting the right colors and how to combine them properly.

Learn Not to Over-Mix

Learn only to mix as much as is necessary for the painting you are working on. When combining colors, mix them as necessary before applying your strokes and lines. When you over-mix colors, your painting becomes a messy pile of uninteresting and inconsistent paint. When you mix correctly, you create a vivid and aesthetically pleasing artwork.

Use As Much Paint As You Desire

Use as much paint as you desire to achieve the perfect painting. Do not hold back on achieving your desired result because you are trying to save up some paints. There are times when you don't require heavy painting. However, certain paintings require heavy strokes, so you have to use enough paint to achieve that. Don't swirl your brush over a thin pool of paint on your palette. Use as much paint as necessary to create a perfect piece.

Use Wet Versus Dry Brush

You need to remember that you can always paint directly on a wet surface and allow it dry, then use damp paint on it again. That way, your color will blend smoothly on the canvas, which is best for getting gradients and transitions. On the other hand, using a dry brush will give your painting a more textural effect, ideal for painting dirt or brick.

Use the Palette Knife

The palette knife isn't only for mixing paint. You can use this tool to create exciting paint strokes on your canvas. Sometimes, you don't always need a paintbrush to create the perfect. Using a palette knife is best for creating unpredictable and textural strokes when painting, which might be challenging to achieve if you use a paintbrush.

Chapter Summary

- Celtic patterns are used to decorate many items such as pendants, necklaces, and rings.

- Carefully balance your color to enhance the aesthetic of your Celtic knotwork

In the next chapter, you will learn line enhancements. See you there!

Chapter Seven:
Line Enhancements

Line enhancement is a unique element in design that accelerates and improves the interface for the users. This doesn't indicate that you have to use this technique for task completion, but it is a method to quicken the design process. Users apply enhancement methods to accelerate their design. It is also referred to as an accelerator or shortcut. There are many ways of enhancing lines in the design. You will learn those methods in this chapter.

How to Add Accents and Symbols

There are many accented letters and symbols available to be included and not limited to l é, ñ, à, ó. The simple way to add emphasis is to use only those symbols that are important to your design. These symbols help to enrich your design. There are two methods of adding accented symbols. You can add it through Adobe Glyphs palette or keyboard shortcuts. I will teach the two methods to add accent and symbol from the comfort of your home.

Add accents and symbols through Adobe Glyphs' palette.

Required Materials

- Computer system

- Adobe InDesign software

Instructions

Follow these simple steps to add your accent and symbols through Adobe Glyphs' palette.

Step 1: Install Adobe InDesign software on your personal computer.

Step 2: Click on Document in Adobe InDesign, then select letter.

Step 3: Select Windows, after you will click on Type and Tables, then open new Glyphs. The Glyphs palette will assist you in getting all the characters available for the font of your choice.

Step 4: Click the glyph you want two times and use it.

Step 5: To add the glyph, right-click on the mouse and choose Add to Glyph Set, then attach your desired glyph.

How to Add Symbol through Keyboard Shortcuts

Materials needed

- Computer system

- InDesign software

- Keyboard

Instructions

Follow these simple steps to add accent and symbol through keyboard shortcuts

Step 1: Click on your InDesign software.

Step 2: Open a new document.

Step 3: Use different shortcuts to input your desired accents and symbols. For instance, to input LowerCase Acute Accent, you will click on ALT+E and instantaneously press the letter A or another vowel you desire on your keyboard. For Upper Case Acute Accent, you will Click on ALT+E, and immediately you will tap SHIFT+A or another vowel of your desire.

How to Add Language Accent Characters

This is one of the most difficult tasks to accomplish, especially for those who use computers. You might find it difficult to modify the accent and character. You will learn step by step methods of adding the language accent character. The Language Accent software can allow for easy addition of these characters and at the same time help you to learn the keyboard shortcuts associated with that character.

Instructions

Follow these simple steps to insert your language accent tool.

Step 1: Turn on the Language Accent tool. You can achieve this by clicking on settings on your InDesign tool. You will see and turn on the Language Accents and other tools to intermediate the design and make it simple.

Step 2: Interface. After turning on your language accent tool, a new language accents button will appear at the down part in the Design Tools sidebar. Click this button to open the Language Accents controls. After clicking on the button, an instruction will pop up.

Using Language Accent Tool to Create Content

After turning on your language accent character tool, you will have to create content with it. Although it may look cumbersome at first, practice from time to time will simplify it. I will teach you this method today.

Instructions

Step 1: Open your design software, click on the editing page, and then press Launch Design Tools.

Step 2: when you get to the Design Tools menu, press the Language Accents button.

Step 3: Choose the language of choice from the pop-up list.

Step 4: Move the mouse cursor to the part where you would like to input an accent character.

Step 5: Tap the button two times for the accent you would like to add.

Step 6: Then, you press the Save button.

The decoration is an essential part of interior design. Decorating with pattern will help you lift your home's face from ordinary to extraordinary and make it look attractive. You can add this pattern to an interior scheme such as the wallpaper, curtains, tiles, and bed linen. Decorating with the use of pattern most times looks like a Herculean task. The actual truth is that if you follow the simple rules, you will be able to add a bold design to your home with confidence.

Floral Pattern

This is a Flower-base design. This design is old fashioned, but it is evergreen. The floral design is suitable for everyone, including those who love a more subtle, abstract floral motif.

Balance

The main essence of adopting a pattern in your home is to achieve balance. You can accomplish this by spreading the design in your room. Concentrating on the pattern in a spot will make it look drab and not attractive. A combination of block colors that go in line with the color available in your design will help achieve the balance. Also, the size of your room determines the type of design or pattern you will use.

A large room should be used for a large design while a small room will be perfect for a small design.

When you are choosing stripes, select the ones that match your room. For instance, a room with greater height will be matched by vertical lines, while a wide room will be attractive with horizontal lines.

Mixed patterns

Mixing patterns create a better impression in the house. Although, using too much color may not make the room look mature. To mix color, you need to experiment with the pattern you have selected. For instance, if you are using floral patterns, try to combine large scale prints with tiny foliage designs. Whichever design you choose, you must include some white and complementary colors into the mix. This will have a total effect on your design.

Geometric

Repetition is the secret tool that makes geometric patterns attractive and exotic. The gorgeous look of the pattern makes us feel safe and content. Another way round, if you fall into a square design, change it with curvy ceramics, soft linens, and organic shapes such as pot plants.

Where Can I Use Patterns?

Patterns can be used in a variety of ways in the living room. It can be used to beautify your soft furniture such as cushions, rugs, and major furniture items such as a sideboard, coffee table, or sofa. This is to reduce the number of designs to a sizable one and balance them with standard colors. For instance, in the bedroom, a designed bed cover can be a decision point to a plain room when used hand in hand with straight colors in sheets and blankets.

A designed tile on the floor can change a utilitarian area into a decorative and beautiful one in the bathroom. The same goes for the kitchen. A well-patterned tile in a plain kitchen can make it look mature and add some personality. When you pick a designed tile for your kitchen or bathroom, make sure you repeat the same color from the pattern in some areas to achieve balance. This may be added through curtains, storage baskets, or towels in the bathroom.

Tropical

This is all about establishing a sense by bush or forest. This design makes it look as if you are going to town with numerous designs with plant imprints. Adding this to the wall brings a sense of beauty and maturity. Include tropical artwork to improve the face of your room. You must have it at the back of your mind that you must not stress your eye by applying too many colors. Instead, use a simple and balanced color for contrast.

Wallpaper

Using wallpaper is another good way to add design to your living space. There are many awesome wallpapers you can choose from out there. Animal prints, forest print, cities, and nature are significant wallpapers used for making a tropical feeling in your living space. However, your budget must also suit every decoration style you choose.

Also, your living space's size should determine the type of wallpaper you are going to select. For instance, a small space should consider ornate wallpaper. Also, placing a paper alcove at the back of shelves or under the kitchen island should be considered. Note that choosing an attractive wallpaper will make your room and other living space a joy to behold.

How to Use Background Patterns in Interior Design

The design placed on your walls, ceilings, and floors can make a special background effect for the room. It will interest you to know that a good background interior design can ameliorate bad architecture design, such as using a vertical stripe to push up the low ceiling and amend lack of a view by choosing a mural. Sometimes you can add or texture to sheetrock walls. However, there is a need to follow the step by step methods to using pattern as a background.

Step 1: Select a design and its color in accordance with the size of the room. To choose the most practical design and color for your room, always have your room's size in the back of your mind.

For small rooms, you should choose a simple colored design with soft backgrounds. For Medium rooms, you can select strong colored designs with simple backgrounds to make the room look spacious, and for the large rooms, pick a strong and serious design with interesting background colors.

Step 2: Pick a design according to its compatibility with the size of the house's style. Try and avoid an old design for a Modern structure. Also, you must consider the basic architectural patterns of your house and your area if available. However, for contemporary rooms, you should use geometric designs with no colors. For old rooms, pick a traditional design, especially those that are based on a historical event.

Step 3: Measure the size of your design to the room size. Make use of small designs in small rooms, normal designs in medium rooms, and large-scale designs in spacious rooms.

Design Rules for Textures and Patterns

Texture and pattern are subtle elements to use. What you can see and touch are very important, so it forms an essential design element. While patterning a room, you should add those elements that improve your experience of space.

Tips on How to Use Texture and Pattern in Your Home

1. Don't downplay the influence of texture and pattern.Both elements are capable of making your room look attractive.

2. You should use textures and patterns to create enough space for a particular purpose or an individual.

3. Use a direct light to improve the quality of the texture.

4. Be careful with how you use high-contrast patterns. It may be disorientating, so use them subtly in your interior.

5. Pick your wallpapers and fabrics with a vertical pattern and then lay more emphasis to allow a better impression of the height.

6. Non-geometric wallpaper may help to create a pseudo effect on the wall when irregularities appear.

7. High designs may attract the attention of the observer towards the pattern, and it is powerful.

8. Select a texture and design to create areas of interest to guide the eye to particular focal points.

Chapter Summary

- Line enhancement improves the aesthetics of Celtic knotworks.

- Creativity and patience are desirable traits for every aspiring Celtic art designer.

In the next chapter, you will learn how to create a Celtic knot decoration.

Chapter Eight:
Create a Celtic Knot Decoration

Celtic designs are beautiful and appealing. People use knots to design their necklaces, jewelry, and fabrics. Come to think of it, the fantastic beauty of Celtic knots is possible because of the stylish pattern of its decoration. Still, nothing but your creativity determines the beauty and attraction of your Celtic knot. Just pay keen attention to how you design your Celtic knot to make it charming and adorable. In this chapter, I will teach you how to create a foldable Celtic knot embellishment.

How to Create a Loop Square

Call it a loop or diamond square, and you're on point. The loop square is beautiful and attractive. Use it to create a striking effect in your home, and you'll love it. How you place the design matters, and you'll need to up your creativity a little bit to make it look perfect. The loop square isn't hard to create. You can do it right there in your home. How? Here is how.

Required Materials

- A pair of scissors

- Glue

- An aluminum finish paper

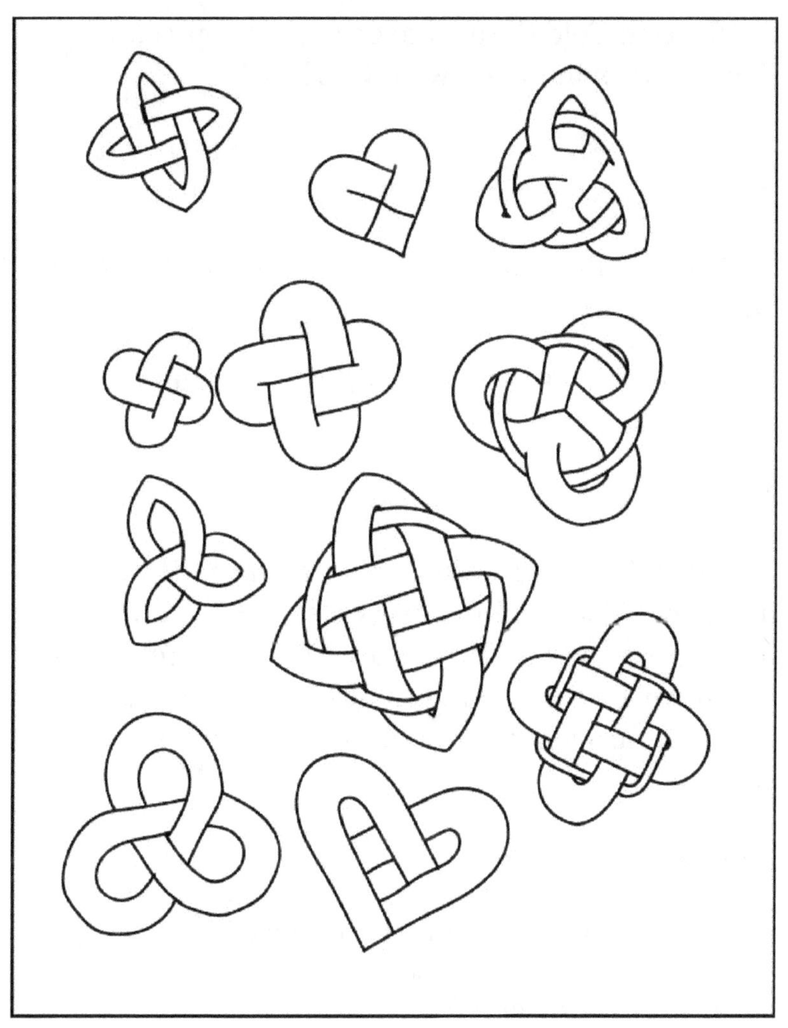

Instructions

Follow these simple steps to create your loop square.

Step 1: Trim your paper a bit and shape each paper's arm to form the base.

Step 2: Fold the arm to back, front, or center, depending on how you want it to look.

Step 3: Swing back the end of each loop and position the center loop in the front of your knot.

Step 4: Raise the arm over the loop and glue ends with the arm.

Crefoil, that's the name of the Celtic knot shape you just designed.

How to Design a Tote Bag

I love Tote bags because they are beautiful and attractive. These colored bags are thrilling, and they are perfect for your loved ones. You can surely design your own Tote bag in the comfort of your home. I will lead you through the process. Here's how to design the bag.

Required Materials

- Two pieces of fabric (vary the color)

- Sewing machine

- Needle

- Thread (according to Needle)

- A pair of scissors

Instructions

Follow these simple steps to design your own Tote bag.

Step 1: Create a body for the Tote bag. Sew the right sides of the fabric together. Stitch the top of the fabrics before you join the seams.

Step 2: Ready two pieces of color-blocked rectangles, cut them into 15" by 17" strips, and join them to the 3 sides of the sewn fabric.

Step 3: Design the lining. Just make sure the lining is a little bit smaller than the exterior part of the bag.

Step 4: Match the corners of the bags while they attach the wrong side of one fabric to the other. Fold the corners to align the bottom and side seam. Watch as a triangle is formed.

Step 5: Leave a few inches above the triangle and stitch on a straight line to create another corner. Hide the corner seam by flipping out the exterior part of the bag.

Step 6: Press the top of the bag a little bit and stitch the interior edge. Cut excess fabric and thread.

How to Design a Celtic Knot with Dots

Dots are great design options for Celtic knots. Creating dots and joining them to design Celtic knots is fun and interesting. Using a few dots to design a Celtic knot will be interesting and worthwhile, although the process may look a little bit complicated. Sure, you can master it and use dots to design a Celtic knot right there in your home. How can I do it? No worries. Here's how.

Required Materials

- Graph paper

- Colored pencils

- Ruler

- An eraser

Instructions

Follow these simple steps to design your own Celtic knot with dots.

Step 1: Sketch a few rectangles of dots. Create even dots on one side of the rectangle while the other side should have odd dots.

Step 2: Locate the diagonal lines pointing to one direction, fill them appropriately, and sketch a few diagonal lines in the other direction facing the previous lines.

Step 3: Join the lines across the walls and those along the corners.

Step 4: Color the spaces within the lines. Feel free you use your favorite colors. Use thick or thin lines to create your Celtic knot.

Step 5: Add extra lines and edges to beautify the knot. Just join the horizontal or vertical dots to create additional edges and lines to spice up the Celtic knot.

Step 6: Erase extra lines and edges.

Artists continue to be inspired to create Celtic knots because of its many lovely designs and iterations. In Celtic mythology, knots symbolize the sacredness of the universe and the elements that hold life firmly. Key and step patterns, including spirals, are tied in a continuous stylized rope, unlike knots' graphical sketches. Again, Celtic knots vary from one another in the areas of complexity and shape, and you might have seen them in ancient manuscripts, local Irish pubs, and tattooed bikers. Sure, these knots add no small beauty to items they embellish. In our robust interactions with established modern Celtic knot designers, we learned a few tricks and twists in the meaning, history, and how to create Celtic knots using Adobe illustrator. Here, I will run through the whole process to easily use these knots for decoration purposes.

Designing a Celtic Knot

Alexander Babich is the manager of MacoshDesign. He confessed that the animated film he watched aided his interest in Celtic knots—the major character stylishly designed amazing Celtic patterns and designs in the film, which enchanted Alexander. So, as time went by, Alexander studied. He studied Celtic designs extensively and later created his personal Celtic designs. He sees the whole thing as solving a crossword and creating something unique and extraordinary. An intricate knot turns out great if you carefully and creatively interlace your strips. For Alexander, place one strip over the loop and another one below it. Find a way to twist the knot and carefully connect the two ends of the strip to attain one infinite line. He called this the magic of Celtic knot design. Here is Alexander's process of creating a Celtic knot.

- Design your backdrop grid: Use your Adobe illustrator to design a vertical A4 document. Click the art board and select 'Rectangular Grid Tool Options.' Change grid weight to 0.1mm while the stroke color remains 0.255.255. Click the illustrator menu to move stroke units from General to millimeters, if it is not already there by default. Use the 'Direction Selection Tool' to create a few vertical and horizontal lines before you push the weight up slightly, from 0.1mm to 0.25mm.

Change the weight of the grid's outer line to 0.35mm. To select the grid, click Selection Tool> Object> Transform> Move and alter the parameters. Get a few copies of the grid. Next, click Selection. Then, Tool> Object> Transform> Move to change the

parameters again. Use these settings to arrive at a 5"
by 5" squares grid.

- Horizontal: 0

- Vertical: 10

- Distance: 10

Click Object> Group to group the squares you are
using to create the outline. Save the grid because you
can use it to design your favorite Celtic pattern and
ornament.

- Adjust the backdrop grid: Sure, you'll need to
  adjust your grid for every ornament you plan to
  design, especially if you're using the same grid
  for your Celtic projects. Just highlight the grid,
  select all, and copy the grid. Use these setting
  parameters.

- Horizontal: 50mm

- Vertical: 0mm

Copy the grid twice to have 4 copies. You can press
Ctrl+D to execute this action. Also, click 'Ellipse Tool'
and locate the intersection of the first horizontal line
and the second vertical line. Sketch your circle from
the intersection point and set width and height to 40
mm. Highlight the circle. Use Ctrl+Shift+M to copy it
six times to arrive at eight circles. Be guided with the

circle if you want to create excellent symmetrical Celtic knots.

- Use your hand to draw the Celtic knot ornament. Start with a few sketches. Just remember that you can't have a perfect drawing. And, what you call imperfections could enhance the aesthetics of your design. Personally, I don't fancy the idea of drawing with a regular pencil. Most times, what you have is just like the ink shade. So, I think a blue pencil is better, although the final decision rests on your shoulders. Again, since Adobe Illustrator can differentiate between drawing with a blue pencil and the regular black ink, you don't need to erase anything before the software can trace your design.

Feel free to do a rough drawing to master the knot you intend to design. Make the drawing accurate as soon as you get the shape you are looking for. Start, center, and end are the three distinct elements of the design. So, endeavor to get it right from scratch, or there will be some issues at the end of the Celtic design. Still, you need to alternate the stripe. Line it top-down to create a striking effect. Also, pay keen attention to the grid when you're dealing with this step. Depending on your color preference, you can use two colors of pens to perfect this stage. To further advance the striking effect, add a few curves and width to your designed stripe.

Use a thin technical pen to trace the knot's edges and a thicker one to perfect the whole drawing. But, if you are confident and composed, use only the thick pen. Scan the drawing or move it to your Adobe libraries through Adobe Capture.

- Use Vector to create a seamless Celtic knot border: Open an Adobe Illustrator document and drag your drawing into the page. Click Image Trace and choose the Black and White tracing style. Feel free to use the settings above. Just make sure that you mark the box close to 'Ignore White' and unmark the one beside 'Strokes.' Next, change the tracing to paths. How? Open the control panel and click 'Expand.' Another way to do this is: click control panel > Object > Image > Expand. Great! Click the Line Segment Tool to sketch two vertical lines. Station the lines in the three elements I already talked about—start, middle, and end elements.

Click the Pathfinder panel to use the options there to enhance your drawing. You can also use Shift+Ctrl+F9 to run this process. Mark the box beside 'Divide and Outline Will Remove Unpainted Artwork' and click 'Ok.' Remember to click 'Divide' in the panel. Ungroup these elements by pressing Shift+Ctrl+G. The Celtic knot is ready but let's add a few details to make it charming and attractive.

- Add details. Just alter the fill to add a few vertical and outline lines. Go through the connection points to select the background you want and scale it up a bit to differentiate thin lines from thick ones. Why? The pattern has to be very clear for people to love it. Copy and print the pattern once you finish designing it. Adopt this pattern for your multiple designs. You could vary your designs by creating a few ropes, enhancing the background with more decorations, initiating shading, or simply by adding a few strokes. However, try to avoid a situation where all the knot's vertical lines connect. Also, a perfect drawing does not exist. What you call imperfections may breathe life on the Celtic knot. Be creative with your decorations so that you can end up with an appealing and colorful Celtic pattern.

Chapter Summary

- Celtic designs are bold and beautiful, and they are used to design necklaces, jewelry, and other fabrics.

- You need to up the level of your creativity to create one.

In the next chapter, you will learn more about Celtic knotted coasters.

Chapter Nine: Celtic Pattern Knotted Coasters

Have a little more yarn left? These coasters are the best way to put those bits and pieces to use. These knots are handy, and the beautiful thing is that they are easy and fun to create.

Carrick Bend Mat Knot

The Carrick bend mat is also known as the thump mat or the more popular Carrick mat. It is a classic Turk's head weave and is related to the Turk's head knot. A Carrick bend-mat knot holds a significant value in some religions due to its interwoven structure.

People use the Carrick bend-knot pattern to create an aesthetically pleasing design on table mats or hot pads. The true Carrick bend is referred to as the full or double Carrick bend because of the eight crossings where each strand of rope passes over and under alternatively.

There are two types of Carrick Bend knots.

1. Single Carrick bend: these are less secure knots, and some examples are the granny, thief and reef knot, the sheet bend, among others.

2. Double Coin Knot: here, the tag end comes out of the same side instead of emerging diagonally.

To create a Kringle mat, follow these steps.

Step 1: Use a 10" cotton cord when making your Kringle mat. Find the middle of the cord.

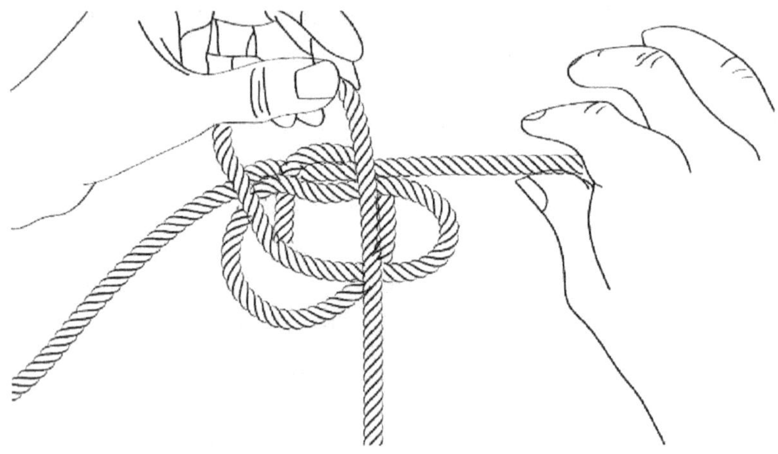

Step 2: Bring the cord's right end over the left and vice versa over three strands. Bring the right end under, then over, and under alternatively, and also make the left end go under, over, and under in the same manner.

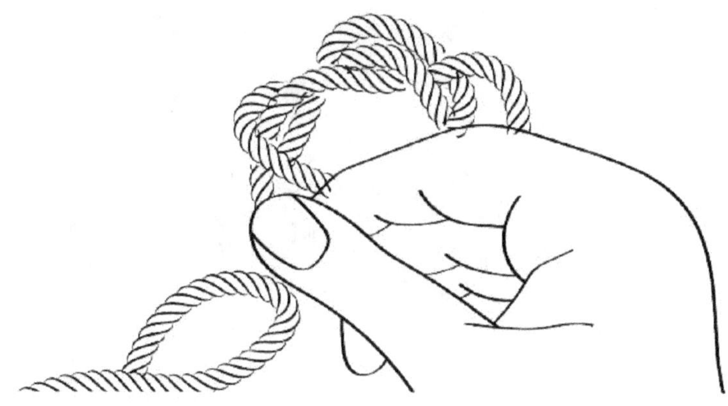

Step 3: Once you have done that, your mat base is set. You could double or trip this by making each end parallel till your knot is complete.

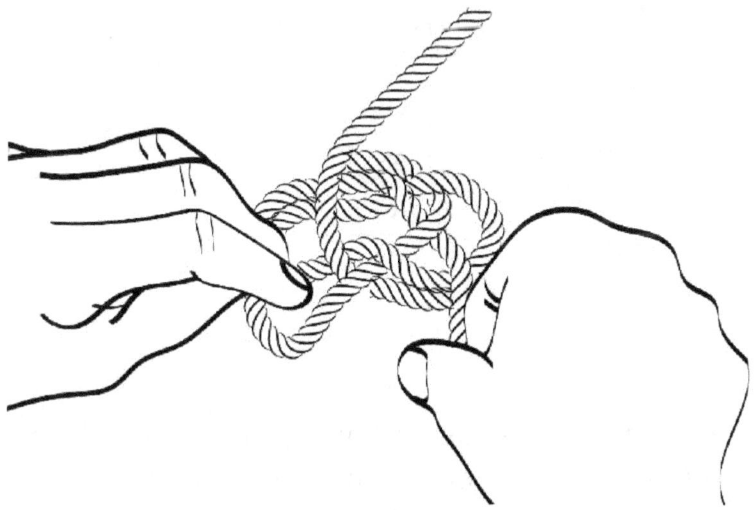

Step 4: Trim off the rough edges.

To make your Carrick bend-mat knot, you can follow these steps.

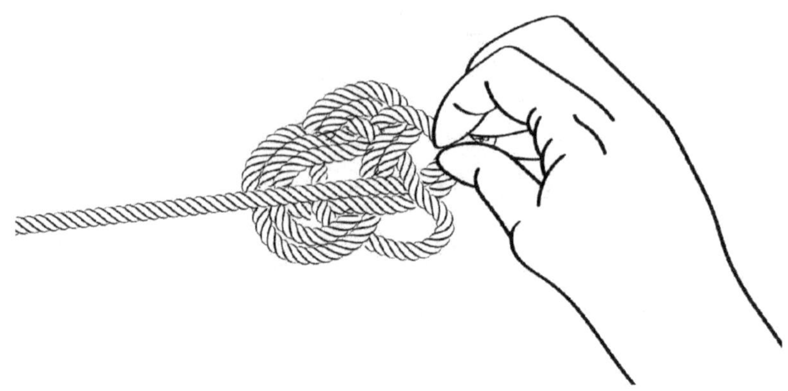

Step 1: Use a 10" out of the cotton cord.

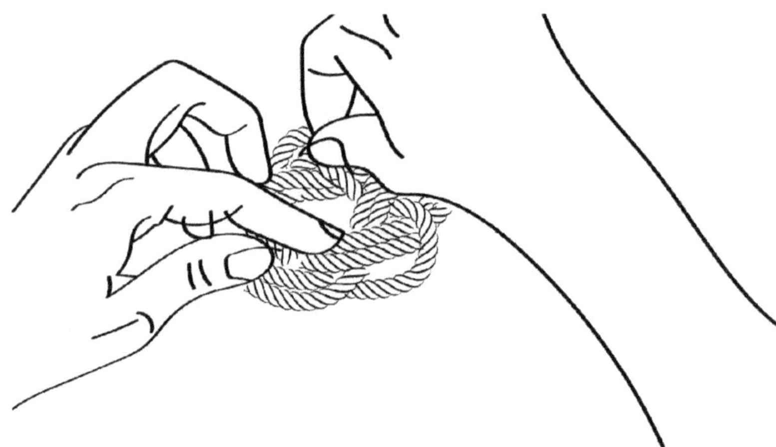

Step 2: Middle the cord and set the right end over the left to create a loop. Continue going over the two strands of the loop you just made, under the left-hand end. Once that is done, your mat base is complete.

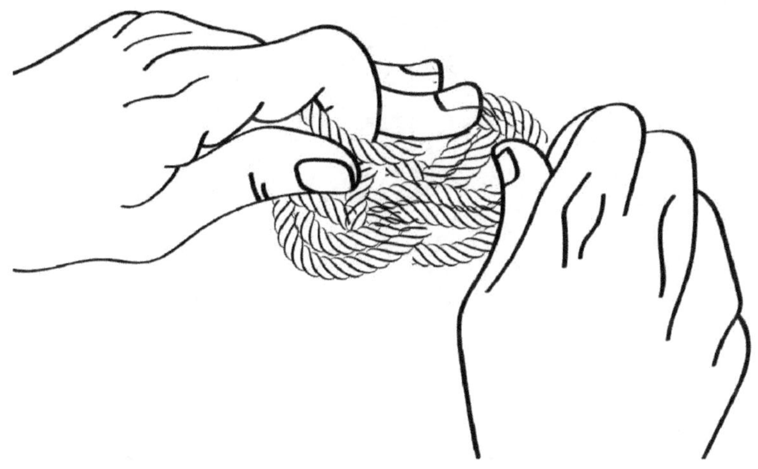

Step 3: Take each end, go parallel to the appropriate strand, tie each strand with a constrictor knot, and trim off any rough edge.

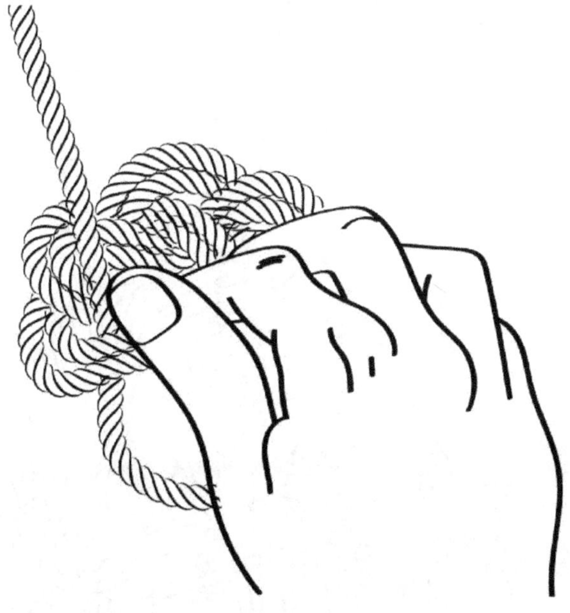

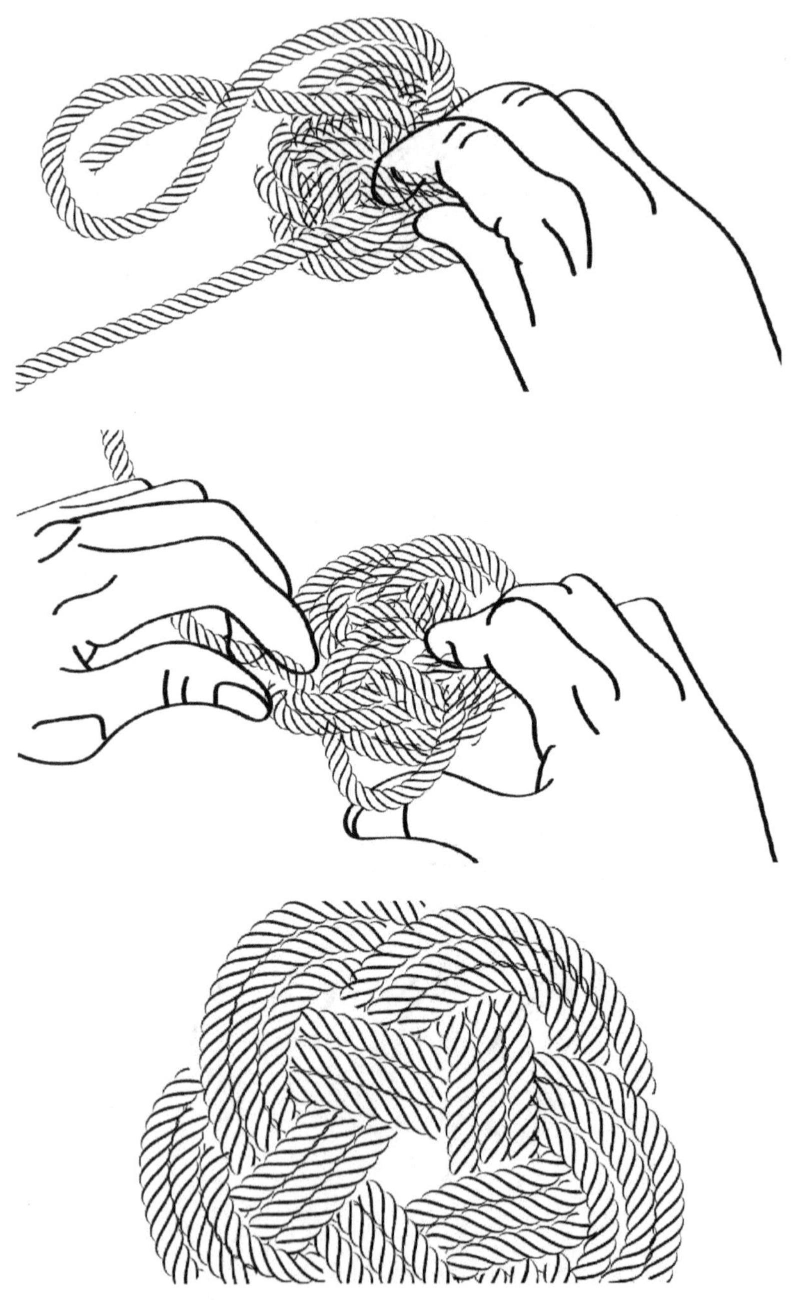

Your Carrick bend mat is complete.

Knots Based on Carrick Bend

The Carrick Mat: The Carrick mat is a decorative woven knot typically used for pads and mats that consists of Carrick connected by their ends to form an endless knot.

Diamond Knot: Starting as a Carrick bend, the diamond knot is tied in a pattern that allows all ends to emerge opposite and parallel to their respective standing point.

Mooring Hitch

The mooring hitch is a simple knot that can be released quickly with just a pull at the tag end. However, it is more secure than the slippery hitch knot, and sailors use it for temporarily mooring boats.

You can tie a mooring hitch around a tree, pole, or anywhere along the length of another rope. Tying a mooring hitch is one of the easiest things to do, and all it takes is just a few steps. These steps are:

Tie a rope to a pole, stick, or tree and pass the string's working end (it can be any of them) through the gap.

- Form a bight with the working end of the rope.

- Pass the bight behind the standing part through the loop created.

- Hold the bight already in the loop and then pull a little to tighten the knot.

- Ensure your release end of the rope is standing out and a bit longer than the other end. Just like that, you have made a Mooring hitch knot.

When you combine the mooring hitch with the butterfly knot, note that it becomes more secure, mostly when used to hold items together.

Friendship Knot

A friendship knot is a beautiful square-shaped and highly secure knot, usually made from other different colors of threads/ropes. It forms part of the eleven essential traditional Chinese knotting craft which originated during the Tang and Song dynasty (960-1279 AD).

Many people use the friendship knot for macramé patterns and tie straps, scarves, ropes, lanyards, ribbons, and paracords. When used on fuzzy or twisted strings, they tend to come out better.

Even in modern times, the friendship knot is very popular, as most scouts and guides are seen wearing their neckerchiefs in a friendship knot style, instead of the usual woggle.

Surprisingly, you may have seen the friendship knot countless without realizing it. Interestingly, the knot symbolizes the World Association of Girl Guides and Girl Scouts (WAGGGS).

You can also find designs of the friendship knots on jewelry, tattoos, and even art pieces. A friendship knot symbolizes the bond and beauty of friendship. It also represents a sign of appreciation.

Getting to tie that scarf, rope, or ribbon of yours in a friendship knot is relatively easy, and here are the easy ways to tie a friendship knot.

- Get two straps of alternating colors (optional). Let's assume these colors are black and white.

- Make sure the size of both ends of the strap is equal. They appear symmetrical that way.

- Cross both straps and pass the black under the white strap.

- Take the white end of the strap and place it end down.

- Place the black strap the same way but facing the right to form the letter' Z.'

- Pass the white through the angular loop formed by the 'Z' of the black strand.

- Hold both ends of the straps and pull to tighten the knot.

- Whip or add some glue to prevent having fraying ends.

- Trim off excesses.

Note: If you're using a rope, it's best to get a stiff one to retain the shape.

Your Friendship knot is complete.

Diamond (Lanyard) Knot

Diamond knot, also known as Bosun's whistle, lanyard, or knife lanyard knot, is an intricate knot used to make a decorative or fixed loop at the middle of a cord, which could be a rope, paracord, lanyard, or even leather.

You can use a diamond knot as your zipper pull to make it more secure. You can also use it to create a macramé pattern. Diamond knot designs can also be found on jewelry designs, key chains, knife tassels, and tattoos. You can create a diamond knot using a single or two ropes (although it's usually better with two strands) and then make them into a single knot.

When you see a finished diamond knot, it may appear challenging to implement, and you'd likely make mistakes at the first trial, but with constant practice, you can be perfect at tying the perfect diamond knot. Making a diamond knot is like making a Carrick bend. With these simple instructions, it becomes easier and faster to tie your diamond knot.

- As a beginner, get 2 ft. of rope.

- Form a ring loop with the rope and encircle the loop with the rope.

- Pass one part of the rope through the loop to create another loop.

- Pass the other end through the newly made loop.

- Take the initial end up.

- Pass it through the first loop.

- Now take the other end through the same loop to create a bigger loop.

- Hold and pull the bigger loop and watch all the loops tighten together.

Just like that, your diamond knot is made.

Scaffold Knot

The scaffold knot is sometimes called the triple overhand noose or gallows knot. It closely resembles the hangman noose because it is also a noose knot. The scaffold knot is made to resemble a noose and form a loop that fits snuggly when tied around any object, rail, or bar.

The scallop knot is almost similar to the poacher's knot (also called two-turn or double scaffold), but the difference is that scallop knots are made with an extra turn around the standing end. You should note that you shouldn't tie the scallop knot or any other noose knot around a person's neck as it could prove to be fatal because the breaking strength of a scallop knot is around seventy-five percent.

Don't let that scare you away, though. You can still make a scallop knot when you go hiking or sailing, especially for lifelines and harnesses. Flathead anglers also use the scallop knot when fishing. You can also use the scallop knot to join two ropes together. Because of how secure the knot is, you can attach the knot to a shackle or carabineer to make it easier when climbing.

Tying a scallop knot is quite complicated, but practice makes perfect. Here are easy steps to create a scallop knot.

- Get your rope. Wrap one end of the rope around the standing bight of the rope.

- Wrap that same end twice around the opposite direction to create a loop. Pass the end over the loop.

- Gently take it out parallel to the standing part. After you have done that, hold the loop and pull the end to tighten the loop.

Your scallop knot is complete. You can add a thimble to ensure your knot lasts longer.

You can always adjust the loop by pulling on the longer end to tighten or loosen the knot. Also, sailors used the thimble to prevent the knot from chafing in boats and yachts, which is why it is recommended that you also use a thimble to protect your knot from wear.

Dropper Loop

The dropper loop, which is also known as a dropper knot, is commonly used by fishermen. Many anglers use the dropper loop for deep-sea or bass fishing because it aids them in creating multiple hook bait rings.

A dropper loop is highly secure and a top fishing knot employed by fishermen because it is often useful to attach rubber worms or tube lures above a jig. Even a moderately strong knot can make a small catch like panfish or tiny saltwater species when fishing.

Here are the ways to tie a dropper loop.

- Get a strand. Create a long loop, hold its top, and wrap it around itself. Wrap the loop five more times.

- Pass the top through the center loop. Pull it and stretch the ends (with your mouth) to make your loop tighter.

- Once it is tightened to your desire, your dropper knot is ready to use.

Another way to create your dropper loop is by keeping your first loop while twisting the other end to a matchstick at an overlapping point. Then slid the bigger loop through the tiny one left by the matchstick to form a dropper.

You should know that the number of times you wrap your loop around the straight line determines how tight and small your dropper will appear. If you created the dropper loop for fishing, you should ensure that you test your knot before setting out to fish.

Make sure your loop is very long if you want to set a hook directly to it and reduce the twisting and fouling rate of your fishing line.

Cat's Paw Knot

Cat's Paw Knot is perhaps one of the easiest to tie. It is used to connect a line or rope to a hook, swivel. People, mostly sailors and those who work in the docks or piers, prefer the Cat's Paw Knot because it doesn't jam and is excellent for lifting heavy loads from an angle.

Why Cat's Paw knot is excellent for lifting things is because of the twisted loops. It is more substantial and secure so that even when one end breaks, the other end holds temporarily till the task is completed.

Fishermen also use the Cat's paw knot for loop to loop connection when fishing. You can use the knot to join a braid to another or a mono leader. The Cat's paw can be directly connected to a Bimini Twist. The knot is mentioned in The Ashley Book of Knots.

Here's how to tie a Cat's Paw Knot.

- Create two loops with a bight of rope. Twist each end of the loops around themselves. Repeat the process three times.

- Bring both loops close to each other. Pass a hook across the center of both loops and pull it to tighten the knot.

Just like that, your Cat's Paw Knot is complete.

You don't necessarily have to make use of a rope bight. You can also make a paracord double line or a closed strop to create the knot. Another thing to note is that certain knot modifications tend to have additional twists on both ends of the rope bight.

Poacher's Knot

Also known as the Strangle snare and double overhand noose, the poacher's knot is a highly secure knot that is mainly used to bind items together. One notable thing about this particular knot is that it can be tied even in very slippery ropes made out of Spectra and Dyneema because other types of loop knots will quickly come undone when tied on these ropes.

Poachers commonly used it for hunting for birds and other small animals. You use the knot to connect a rope to a carabiner as a hitch or part of a snag. Cat paw's knot can also be used to form a simple snare. Along with the scaffold knot, the poacher's knot can be made stronger and is ideal for tying a foot loop to a hand ascender.

Here's how to Tie a Poacher's Knot.

- Wrap the tag end around a rope bight. Repeat the process once, take it up, and pass it through the two loops.

- Pull both ends of the loop to tighten the knot.

Do not make the mistake of making just one turn around the standing part. When you do that, you're only making an ordinary overhand knot, which isn't strong enough to lift heavy objects. If there is enough tag, you can add a stopper knot for more strength and security.

Hangman's Knot (Noose)

The hangman knot or noose, as the name indicates, was used originally for the execution of prisoners. It is believed to have been invented in the United Kingdom. Recently, its uses have diversified for fishing and boating. Anglers use the knot to attach a swivel, lure, or hook to their fishing line. Sailors and hikers also use the knot to tie down a boat, tent, or vehicle because of its self-tightening quality.

People like to make it for Halloween decorations and other artistic purposes. The knot is also employed when making bracelets and paracord knife lanyards. The loop formed by the strong knot is adjustable.

Remember, never use this knot on any human, whether in a playful manner or not, because the loop could tighten accidentally even when tied loosely and can prove fatal.

Knowing that, let's get into the process of creating a Hangman's knot. Here is how you can tie a Hangman's knot/noose.

- Make an '8' shape with your rope and pass the tag end behind the '8' form you made.

- Then wrap the end around the upper loop and the standing part of the rope. Repeat the process three times.

- Pass the stationary part through the small top loop. Hold the lower loop and pull the tag end to tighten the loop.

After that, your Hangman's knot is complete.

Butterfly Knot

Also referred to as the Alpine Butterfly knot or Lineman's Loop, the Butterfly knot is used mainly for rock climbing and glacier travel because it holds the climber in the middle when two or more people move up a rope.

It is also used to attach a carabiner to the climbing harnesses. There is also the Double Butterfly Knot, which is quite similar to the regular butterfly knot, but the difference is that the knot has two side by side loops instead of one.

Double butterfly knot offers the same highly secure knot since it has the advantage of providing two slip points instead of one. The Butterfly knot is regarded as one of the most secure knots, and it is also one of the easiest to tie.

Following just three simple steps, you have completed the Butterfly knot, and these steps are:

- Form an '8' shaped loop and fold the upper loop down. Pull it around and pass the upper loop through the lower loop.

- Pull both loops to tighten the knot.

You just made a butterfly knot.

Valdotain Tresse

People used this knot initially in Alpine rescue, from where it graduated into being a famous arborist knot. Climbers use the VT knot to ascend and descend ropes when climbing. Valdotain Tresse is used to attach a carabiner to a climbing rope. It is also best for rock climbing and caving. You can use the VT knot for canyoneering and when engaging in technical rescue activity. The knot is also great as a rappel device, and you can use the knot for slacklining.

One unique thing about the VT knot is that you can always release the knot under load. Tying a Valdotain Tresse knot isn't a small feat for a beginner because it could cause death or other severe damage to people and property if not appropriately secured. Hence extra care needs to be taken when making a Valdotain Tresse. You must follow guidelines for tying the knot to ensure that there is no mistake.

The VT knot can be with a rope with two sewn or spliced eyes (or split tail friction cord) or hand-tied loops. Here are the steps on how to tie a Valdotain Tresse.

- Wrap both tag ends around your rope bight.

- Pass it through the two loops created. Pull both ends to tighten.

- Wrap the right end loop four times around the blue rope. Pass the blue rope down from the backside.

- Wrap it once around the red rope again. Wrap the left end of the red rope around the blue rope.

- Pass both ends through a carabiner.

- Close the carabineer to complete the knot.

Once you make your VT knot, test its effectiveness using different diameters, lengths, and friction cord materials. One interesting fact about the VT knot is that step one to three are also the same way you can make a Poacher's knot.

Chapter Summary

- Celtic pattern coasters are the best way to put those bits and pieces to good use.

- They are handy, beautiful, and fun to design.